PRESENCE
DRIVEN

PAUL ELLIS

ISBN
978-1-958690-55-0 (Paperback)
978-1-958690-56-7 (eBook)
978-1-958690-54-3 (Hardcover)

Table of Contents

Foreword

AS I READ PAUL'S BOOK, this Scripture came to my mind:

*"I saw the Spirit come down from heaven as a dove, and it remained on Him.
I would not have known him except that the One who sent me to baptize with
water told me, 'The man on whom you see the Spirit come down and remain
is He who will baptize with the Holy Spirit.'"*
(John the Baptist in John 1:32-33).

This is what Paul is writing about. Everything has a purpose, but it is only
when the purpose and the presence come together that we can experience
the power of God at work. The initial thought that the Holy Spirit gave to
Paul was, "Without my presence, your purpose has no reason."

Paul takes us on a journey through some of our favorite Bible stories
and shows us the unfavorable consequences of pursuing purpose without
presence. Then he turns it around and shows us the outcome that happens
when purpose and presence come together. The great miracles in the Bible
and the stories of men and women of faith are the fruit of purpose and
presence coming together and forming a perfect union.

In each of the four Gospels, the Holy Spirit is depicted as a dove. It was
a dove that came upon Jesus Christ at His baptism. The dove is a shy,
sensitive bird. Maybe this is why the Apostle Paul wrote, "Do not grieve
the Holy Spirit" (Ephesians 4:30). In this book, you will see what happens
when the Holy Spirit is grieved, disconnecting the presence from purpose.
When this happens, purpose becomes a struggle, and the walk of faith
becomes a walk of work.

As Paul goes through the Bible stories, he shows us that there is no limit to
what can be done when the purpose is presence driven. He shows you that

faith is the key to retaining the connection between presence and purpose and that we must love the Promiser more than the promises.

"Presence Driven" unfolds a revelation that we need to be able to live empowered and purpose driven lives that produce miraculous results.

Larry Neville
President Praise Chapel International
larry@praisechapel.com

Words of my mouth—
Meditations of my heart

PRESENCE DRIVEN

Preface

KING DAVID WROTE IN PSALM 19:14, "Let the words of my mouth and the meditations of my heart be acceptable to You, O Lord, my strength and my redeemer."

David's desire was that the Lord would approve of, find pleasure in, and be pleased with what he thought about; the secret thoughts and imaginations of his heart. And that He would approve of what David said, as well as, how he "said it."

In Psalm 119:18, David would ask the Lord to show him wonderful and marvelous things from His Holy Word.

His prayer was that the Lord would bring revelation to him from His Word and that he would, be able to see it. But we know that in our humanity, we are capable of seeing something and still not understanding what we've seen.

This is why David asks the Lord in verse twenty-seven of the same chapter, to allow him to understand, or in other words, to receive revelation concerning the things the Lord had shown him.

The Psalmist here didn't just ask the Lord to "see" the things of God, but he asked Him to enable him to understand them. He finishes verse 27 by stating that once he saw and understood, then, he could talk about it.

We cannot talk about what we don't understand with clarity or confidence, although I'm certain that we've all made this mistake. And it doesn't take an optometrist to see the error.

Presence Driven is the first installment in the series: **Words of my mouth… Meditations of My Heart.** My greatest desire in ministry is to provoke the Church of Jesus Christ to passionately pursue Him in these three areas.

1. To have passion for the Lord.
2. To have passion for His Word.
3. To have passion for His presence.

As we walk together through the pages of this book, I pray that they will inspire you to pursue these three passions, and they will enable you to apprehend God; and everything that He has for your calling, destiny, legacy, and life.

In December 2009, my father went home to be with the Lord. After his passing, the church that my wife, Val, and I were assistant pastors of thought it would be a good idea to send us on a trip to Nadi, Fiji, for what they termed 'a little bit of ministry and a whole lot of relaxation.'

On our last day in Nadi, we were at our dear pastor friend's home, worshipping the Lord together.

The presence of the Lord was strong that evening. There was an almost electric atmosphere of the Lord's glory that had come into the house. In his prayer, our pastor friend said to the Lord, "Let us be presence driven." As soon as those words left his mouth, the Holy Spirit ignited them in my soul: and the Lord spoke (as a matter of fact) to me, saying, "You must be presence driven." He continued, "Understand this: you can have purpose without presence, but you cannot have presence without purpose."

Finally, He said to me, "I don't want my Church to just be purpose driven; but with their purpose, I want them to be presence driven; because purpose cannot be achieved without presence. Without presence, your purpose has no reason."

Everyone, who has ever been born, has been born with purpose—everyone. However, purpose alone will never be a vehicle that drives a man to fulfill his destiny.

I understand that everything that exists has a reason for its existence. If it ceases to have a reason, it ceases to exist. I am confident that you can think of things in your lifetime that at one time had a purpose, a reason. But for whatever reason it could be, maybe because technology has advanced, or there was a shift in the market, or even simple economics; they were either discontinued or in some way phased out.

They became obsolete and, as a result, lost their reason to exist. We may have a purpose, even a Kingdom purpose: but without His presence, our purpose has no reason, and it ceases to exist, or we spend our lives going through the empty motions of what existence should be.

In these next few chapters, it is my desire to give you a few selected examples from the Bible of some who had purpose without presence and for us to see the result.

I also want you to see what took place when their purpose connected to the Lord's presence: how those callings were fulfilled, destinies were shaped, and legacies were left as a testimony of the Lord's power when purpose meets presence.

Chapter One

Presence Lost...

THE FIRST ESTABLISHMENT OF THE standard of purpose being connected to presence happened in the garden with Adam. Adam was created with purpose, and he was created in the presence.

The Bible says in Genesis 2:7 that God formed Adam from the dust of the ground and then breathed into him; thus, Adam became a living soul. God initiated breath, a breath that would subsequently enable and sustain the life of mankind.

Gen2:8 says that the Lord then planted a garden in an Eastern section of an area known as Eden, and then He placed Adam in this garden.

According to Gen.1:26, 1:28, and Gen.2:15, Adam's purpose was threefold:

ADAM'S FIRST PURPOSE

Adam's first purpose was to have dominion over the earth and all its creatures. The word "dominion," from Hebrew, means to rule. This meant that the first of Adam's purposes was to be the earth's ruler. He was the highest authority, the highest ruling power dwelling on the Lord's earth. He was to govern it in its entirety.

ADAM'S SECOND PURPOSE

Adam's second purpose was to dress the garden. The word "dress" comes from a Hebrew word meaning to work, tend, and cultivate the garden, which was Adam's role. This does not mean that Adam cleared land, tilled earth, irrigated soil, planted seeds, and worked Eden's fields.

Gen.3:17 would suggest to us that this kind of labor came as a result of sin.

Interestingly, "dress" from Hebrew has another meaning. "Dress" also means "to worship." The garden's primary purpose was to be a place of worship for Adam and Eve, and Adam's primary purpose in the garden was to prepare it as a place of worship.

It was to be a place where God's presence would meet Adam's purpose, and the result would be a release of the person, the Word, the glory, the presence, and the fullness and goodness of God. It would be a place of uninhibited fellowship between the God of heaven and His created son.

Adam's primary purpose was to create, prepare, and establish an atmosphere in the garden, through worship, that would attract the presence of the Lord, causing him to anticipate the time when He would come down in the cool of the day and have communion, fellowship with Adam and Eve.

Adam was to make the garden a place of romance. A few years ago, I was leaving a church service in San Diego, CA. As I walked across the street to my car, I looked up into the nighttime sky, and I began to tell the Lord how much I loved Him and thanked Him for His goodness in my life. Suddenly, the Lord spoke into my spirit and said, "I love the courtship process. Don't cheat me out of it."

It was here that God began to reveal to me that He is a very romantic God; and that He loves to romance His Church. This concept of God being a romantic God might seem strange to you: maybe you've never thought of God being a romantic God—but the concept of Him being romantic, even hopelessly romantic, is woven throughout the Bible from Genesis to Revelation. He can't really help Himself; you know? Romancing and being romanced is a part of His very nature, and it is the great desire of His heart.

In fact, if you stop and think about it, the Church is espoused to the Lord. We are currently in the courtship process with Him. One day, He, the

Bridegroom, will come for His Bride, but until then, He courts us, and we respond accordingly.

If you were to think of God's perfect place of romance, what kind of place would come to mind? What do you suppose it would be?

The Bible is indeed very clear in the fact that God has a favorite place of romance. His location of choice to romance His Church is…in a garden.

After He created Adam and Eve, He placed them in and romanced them in a garden in Eden.

Adam and Eve were an Archetype or a foreshadowing of the Church. And just like God came down and romanced them in Eden's garden, the Apostle John said that Jesus, who is God, came down, became flesh, and romanced His created sons.

Jesus had a purpose: to romance "as many as would receive Him and believe in His name." John said that Jesus gave those who believed and received Him the power: the right and legal authority to become sons of God. Jesus' entire earthly ministry: His teaching, preaching, miracles, healings, etc., was a ministry of romance.

Similarly, Adam was the representation of Christ and Eve, the Church. Adam romanced Eve in the Garden of Eden, a shadowing of Christ romancing the Church in the Garden of Gethsemane. In the Songs of Solomon, the Shepherd (another embodiment of Christ) romanced the Shulamite woman (another portrayal of the Church) in a garden.

In Mark Ch.6, Jesus romanced over five thousand men and women at a fish and bread picnic in an area described as a garden. In Luke 16, Abraham's Bosom from the Greek is described as a garden. After His death, Jesus descended into Abraham's Bosom, where for three days He romanced the Old Testament saints and ultimately took them from this garden into His heavenly one. The Apostle Paul said in 2Cor.12:2 that he was caught up into the third heaven, which he called the paradise or the garden of God.

ADAM'S THIRD PURPOSE

Adam's third purpose was to "keep" the garden. The word "keep" from Hebrew meant to guard, protect, hedge about, be aware of, and observe. Adam's purpose in keeping the garden was to vigilantly and diligently be on guard. He was to be constantly looking for and be aware of potential threats and prevent their intrusion into this perfect environment prepared for the worship and presence of God. This was to ensure that its purity would not become polluted or its integrity compromised.

Simply put, Adam was to keep what belonged to the garden inside the garden and keep everything else out. The words dominion, dress, and keep all define Adam's purpose. Adam's purpose and God's presence were in perfect harmony until Adam let down his guard, and the serpent, subtly and craftily, slithered in.

Have you ever wondered why the serpent engaged Eve instead of Adam when Adam was the earth's governor, dresser, and keeper? Why did he "waste" time with a middleman? I believe the answer can be found in what their roles signify. Adam was the governor, the dresser, the keeper—and Eve was his "help-meet."

The term "help-meet," from Hebrew, can be defined as the one who keeps or protects the anointing. Adam was anointed governor of the earth and given dominion over it, and Eve was anointed as Adam's help-meet: she was the one given the charge of protecting Adam's anointing. It was Eve's position to protect Adam's dominion over the earth as well as his responsibility to dress and keep the garden. I believe that is why women are more intuitive and perceptive than men. Women can see things in other people that men often miss.

In my life, there have been numerous times that Val would caution me concerning certain individuals and situations. And she was always right! Why? God created her to be my help-meet. I believe the serpent's strategy to be fairly straightforward. If he could compromise Eve, he could destroy Adam's anointing. Adam would go from having purpose with presence to having purpose without presence, and the result would be the knowledge of evil.

The serpent was not native to the garden. It was a foreign presence that violated and defiled the garden's very environment and polluted its atmosphere. When Eve discovered the serpent's presence, she should have exposed it per her responsibilities as protector of Adam's anointment. And it was Adam's responsibility to neutralize its threat. Well, as we know, she didn't, and he didn't. Can you imagine what kind of world this could have been if Adam had crushed the nasty serpent's head and thrown its vile carcass out of the garden instead of standing passively as his wife was tempted? If only…

FAVORITE FRAGRANCES

Do you have a favorite fragrance? Many of us (myself included) have a perfume or a cologne that we particularly enjoy. Every time we smell it, we breathe in deeply, allowing it to fill our lungs and, simultaneously, our senses. God definitely has a favorite fragrance. It's a fragrance that attracts His presence like no other. However, this fragrance doesn't come from New York, London, or Paris: you'll not find it in a designer bottle, or see it being sold in finer stores such as Nordstrom's, Saks, or Harrods.

Although what they make and sell may smell wonderful to us, the Lord is not impressed. They cannot compete with the fragrance that attracts the Lord's presence: to him alone, it is wonderful!

As Adam prepared the garden for the presence, the Lord released part of what He is, the fragrance of heaven, into the garden. The aroma of His grace, mercy, love, and beauty was upon Adam and Eve, and it would fill the garden with heaven's scent. But not even heaven's scent is the fragrance that is most attractive to God.

Several years ago, my wife and I were pastoring a church in Northeast Nevada. On a daily basis, I would arrive at the church early in the morning and spend the first couple hours of my day with the Lord in worship and His Word. One particular Sunday morning, as I was in a time of worship, suddenly, there was a fragrance that began to fill the sanctuary. It was so clean and fresh and really wonderful. I walked throughout the sanctuary filling my lungs to capacity, inhaling and exhaling repeatedly. What a marvelous experience it was!

I can only imagine what it must have been like when the wind of heaven began to blow into the garden gently, and Adam's sense of smell caught the first whiff of His presence, igniting the rest of his senses. His thoughts and emotions became driven by excitement and anticipation of an encounter with His Father and everything contained in His presence. And when the Lord would depart, the residue left behind of His aromatic beauty remained.

Before the fall, Adam and Eve had the fragrance of heaven on them. It surrounded them. But after the fall, heaven's fragrance lifted from them and was replaced by the smell of death.

While God loves the fragrances, odors, and perfumes of heaven as they are part of who He is, there is one fragrance; one odor that trumps them all. So, what is the smell that captivates the attention of God of heaven like no other? Are you sure you're ready for it? Here it is—It is the smell of death! Does that shock you that God would be so attracted to the aroma of death?

Think with me for a moment. In Gen. 2:17, God said to Adam and Eve that the day they would choose to eat of the fruit of the tree of knowledge of good and evil, they would "surely die." Well, they did eat it, and they indeed died.

It was the smell of death that came on them that caught the Lord's attention on this particular day. This unmistakable smell of death caused Him to come down to the garden to investigate where this smell was coming from. It was the smell of death that caused the Lord to curse the serpent, Adam, Eve, and the earth: but it was also His insatiable attraction to the smell of death that caused Him to declare the promise in Gen.3:15 when He said that the seed of a woman would crush the serpent's head.

It was the smell of death, the sacrificial offerings of bulls, rams, goats, and lambs that attracted the Lord and released grace on the one who offered such sacrifices.

God was attracted to the death of His Son, the Lamb of God, on the cross. Jesus' death attracted the presence in a way that, to this point, had never been imagined, much less realized. When the presence of God came down at Christ's death, He released life on whosoever received and believed in Him.

The same thing applies when we die to ourselves, to our flesh. He must come down and investigate the death of everyone who says to Him, "Lord, I am yours. Not my will, Lord, but Your will. You must increase, and I must decrease. Here I am, Father, I am crucified with Christ; I am not my own. You are my Lord." Jesus must first be known as Lord before He will ever be known as Savior.

When God smells the death of our flesh, He cannot help Himself: the desire to come to the place of sacrifice, this dying to self, cannot be controlled but must be sought out. And when He finds it, He removes the odor of death and replaces it with who He is…the fragrance of heaven.

WHAT'S IN A NAME?

At this point, God had expelled Adam and Eve from the garden. The curses had been positioned, and He had given the promise of recovery as stated in Gen 3:15. God had said that the seed of a woman would crush the serpent's head. They believed that the crushing of the serpent's head would result in the recovery of the garden: and all that was lost would be restored; the nightmare they had woken up to would finally be over.

This promise had shown itself like a shaft of light through the dark and ominous clouds that had gathered due to the curse. All that mattered to them was the recovery of the garden, of their innocence, and of the presence. It began to consume their thoughts and conversations. It was what they looked for, dreamed about, planned for, and prepared for.

How do I know this? How do I know how they felt about where they were and how they planned to recover the garden? It is evident in the meanings of the names of their two sons, Cain and Abel.

> Abel's name means: to be led astray, vain expectations, worthless, empty, vain, void, unsatisfactory, and transitory. Abel's name defines how they felt after having their eyes "opened" knowing good and evil. They had been led astray, tricked, and deceived. What they expected was not what they got! And what they got was unacceptable and unsatisfactory.

They were outside the garden, and what they now saw compared to what they had seen was described in Abel's name: worthless, empty, void...and they hoped that it was only transitory and temporary.

Adam and Eve had lost focus on everything that God had said to them relating to the curse of sin, except for the Lord's promise in Gen.3:15. Their hope of recovering all that they lost is evidenced in the meaning of their other son's name, Cain.

> The name Cain means: to mourn, to lament, to wail as though you're at the funeral of someone that was very dear and precious to you. Think about how you would feel (or how you felt) losing the person or thing that was most precious to you. Imagine life without them. Devastation! You weep, but weeping can't restore what was lost. So, you're left with only memories of the good times and the regrets of poor choices.

This describes how Adam and Eve felt when they had been driven from the garden; when they found themselves with only purpose and no presence. But the meaning of Cain's name doesn't stop there. It also means to strike fast with a decisive, crushing blow, and to recover. Adam and Eve surely thought Cain was to be the fulfillment of God's promise of recovery in

Gen.3:15. In their minds, all their hopes and dreams of recovering the garden, recovering their position, and recovering the presence depended on Cain and his ability to crush the serpent's head.

PRESENCE MUST BE THE MOTIVATION OF OUR PURPOSE

As far as Adam and Eve were concerned, Cain had purpose. I believe that as Cain grew, they groomed, coached, taught, developed, and trained him with one point of focus; with one goal forever seared in his mind— recovering the garden and the presence that was lost.

Why do I believe this? Because of Eve's declaration concerning Cain's birth recorded in Gen 4:1. "Adam knew his wife Eve, and she conceived and bore Cain, and Eve said, 'I have gotten a man from the Lord.'"

> The Hebrew word for "man" here means: a champion, a great and mighty man, a warrior, a worthy man (opponent).

Eve believed that Cain was the fulfillment the promise in Gen. 3:15. Abel's name described their present condition, but Cain would be the one whose purpose would be to strike fast, crush, and recover.

I can imagine that all of Cain's life, Adam and Eve would tell him things like "Son, you were born for this. It's your destiny, your purpose. Nothing else matters, son. No one else matters. Focus, son, stay focused on your purpose. You cannot fail us, you must win. You must crush the serpent's head, you must! It's going to hurt a little, but remember what the Lord said—it will only be like a bruise on your heel. You'll crush its head! You'll be fine! You will win! You must recover the garden! You must. Stay focused, son, focused…"

I also can imagine that they would recount to him, word for word and complete with emphasis, God's promise of a redeemer that would recover the garden and all that they had lost. I believe that Adam and Eve had convinced themselves that Cain not only had the answer to their problem, but that he was the answer. After all, he, unlike Abel, had purpose. Cain's problem was not that he lacked purpose, but that he lacked presence.

By verse three of Gen.4, Cain and Abel had grown up. Cain was indeed a roughneck, a champion, a fighter, a warrior, and a great and mighty man. The will to fight, even to the death, had long been instilled in him. The years of training, developing, and sharpening his skills as a fighter—with only the thoughts of his purpose moving through his mind. Truly, Cain believed himself to be a formidable and worthy opponent.

To Adam, Eve, and especially Cain, Abel became what his name implied: void, empty, worthless, vain, unsatisfactory, and temporary. Cain was the man. He was a man's man, and he knew it. Nothing else—no one else mattered or held his position. Abel was a simple shepherd tending a few sheep, but Cain was a one-man war machine. He was trained mentally, physically, and emotionally: he was programmed to fight, win, and recover.

OFFERING TIME

Abel was a shepherd and Cain was a tiller of the ground. At an appointed time, they both brought an offering to the Lord. Abel brought a lamb, and Cain brought a fruit and vegetable tray.

The Bible says in Verse four that God respected the offering of Abel: He honored Abel by accepting his offering. But verse five says that God did not honor nor accept Cain's offering.

For most of my life growing up in the Church, I was taught, and assumed, that the reason God didn't accept Cain's offering was because Cain brought the produce of the ground and according to Gen.3:17, the ground was cursed, therefore, Cain's offering was cursed. We assume that God respected and accepted Abel's offering because of the shedding of blood. God demonstrates this by using the skins of slain animals to cover Adam and Eve's nakedness and as a testimony of the Lamb of God shedding His blood and giving His life for our sin and covering our nakedness. And there is probably some merit to that.

But, as I read more thoroughly, I discovered that there was a curse on the serpent, man, woman, the ground. This curse obviously affected the Animal Kingdom as well because, after the fall and the establishment of the curse, the same lions, tigers, and bears that Adam and Eve used to converse and play with now saw them either as a threat or as a food source.

Besides that, when God gave Moses the law, He incorporated the produce of the "cursed" ground along with bulls, goats, rams, lambs, etc., in various sacrifices and offerings. The curse affected the whole earth either directly or indirectly. From this perspective, the lamb Abel brought was as cursed as the produce Cain brought. The Apostle Paul said in Galatians 3:13 that just as Abel's lamb was cursed as the result of sin, Jesus, the Lamb of God, was made a curse for us so that through Him, we could be redeemed from the curse.

God accepted Abel's offering because Abel not only had purpose, but he also had the presence. Conversely, I believe that God rejected Cain's offering because he lacked presence, although he had purpose. Abel was humble and dependent on grace; Cain was arrogant and entitled.

God rejected Cain's offering solely because he did not have the presence even though he had a purpose. And because he lacked presence, he brought an offering of produce, which he should have; but what he failed to do was to place his heart upon that tray along with the produce he grew.

God respected Abel's offering primarily, if not entirely because he sacrificed his heart along with his lamb. Abel had a purpose, but he also had what all of Cain's physical, mental, and emotional training and purpose lacked… Abel had the presence.

The Lord admonished Cain to do what was right, and Cain rejected the Lord's counsel. He became angry at God, and bitter jealousy raged within him toward Abel. He was the man while Abel was an inconsequential nothing! I believe that this is the reason that he became so angry. All of his life, he was told by his parents that he was the man and when he came to offer God his produce, he came with an 'I'm the man' arrogance and attitude. And God rejected his offering as if God was saying to him, "No,

Cain, you're not the man, nor will you ever be. Abel is more of a man than you'll ever be." He's refusal to acknowledge Cain as the man caused uncontrollable anger to rise up inside of him.

Well, we know what happened next, don't we? Cain left the presence again, found his brother, overpowered him, and killed him. Then he tried to cover up his sin by hiding Abel's body in the earth.

Please allow me to interject an observation here. Many times, when someone is driven by purpose without the presence, instead of pursuing the presence, they get angry, become bitter, and jealous toward the one who lets presence drive their purpose, as in the case of Saul and David.

The Bible says in Gen.4:9 that the Lord came to Cain and asked him where Abel was.

I think it is kind of funny, in an odd way, that of the first seven questions asked in the Bible, the serpent asked the first, God asked the next six. And it wasn't until Cain asked God his now infamous question concerning being his brother's keeper that a person posed any of those questions.

As I thought about this, it occurred to me that maybe, just maybe, Adam and Eve should probably have asked more questions: and, perhaps, got some clarification on a few things that they might not have quite understood.

In my lifetime, I have been asked and, in turn, have asked many questions. Some of them were good, and some, not so much. But there is one question, from one source, that I pray is never asked of me. I never want the Lord to come to me and ask me the same question that He asked Eve in Gen.3:13 and Cain in Gen.4:10.

The question is, "What have you done?"

Oh, just the thought of Him asking me that question makes me shudder! You know that there will not be an all-expense paid trip to Disneyworld after answering a question like that.

In Cain's blind and jealous rage, he couldn't see that the Lord already knew the answer to the question. He knew exactly what had happened to Abel and where he was. You see, the Lord had never, nor will He ever, lose anything that belongs to Him.

Gen.4:11-15 records the curse placed on Cain as a result of purpose without the presence, and verse sixteen says, "And Cain went out from the presence of the Lord, and dwelt in the land of Nod, of the east of Eden." This is the third time Cain left the Lord's presence. Notice, not one time did the presence leave Cain; he left the presence.

Nod means wandering. We become a "vagabond" Christian when we have purpose with no presence. Our purpose can take us on a journey with no direction; it can become nothing more than aimless movement: and never have established roots.

We live our lives ever moving but going nowhere:

- Never accomplishing our calling.
- Falling short of our destiny.
- Leaving a legacy written in the sand and wiped away by the waves of time.

From this point, Cain continued to live his life with purpose, but he forever lacked presence, and the result was that his legacy remains forever connected to the curse and his generations lost in the flood.

Pause here and think for a moment about Adam and Eve. What has just happened? Can you imagine what they must have been thinking and feeling at this point? How could this have happened? They were so sure, so confident. All the years spent teaching, training, investing, believing. Gone…

Can you imagine their disappointment, their devastation? All that they placed their hopes and dreams in was gone. It was gone! Their hope of recovering the garden, gone! Abel, gone! Cain, gone! Imagine as they peered into subsequent generations and saw the consequences of their choice to disobey God on that fateful day.

In Gen.5:1, the Bible says that Adam knew Eve again, and she bore a son, and they named him Seth. The name Seth means Substituted. Seth became a substitute for Abel, but he could never replace nor recover him. The 5th chapter of the Book of Genesis shows the grim reality of having purpose without presence. It reads as an epitaph written on the headstones of the graves in a genealogical cemetery—each one concluding with the phrase "And he died…"

Chapter Two

Birthing Ishmaels

LONG BEFORE ABRAHAM AND SARAH had the presence, they had purpose. Their purpose is recorded in Gen.12. In this chapter, Moses wrote that God was making a marvelous covenant them. God had called Abraham and Sarah to leave their country, their people, and to go on a journey with Him to a land that they had not seen, which He had promised to show them. Contained in the covenant that God had made with them was a promise that they would birth a great nation. They would be chosen people, selected by God Himself for His purpose.

God promised that His blessing would be on them and their descendants, and in turn, because of the blessing that was on them from the Lord, they would be a blessing to all of the families of the earth.

With purpose established, Abraham and Sarah set out on a journey with God, whose presence would lead them not only to a promised inheritance but toward the fulfillment of their destiny; and to a place where they would establish an everlasting legacy for the benefit of those of us who would succeed them. Although their journey was not without its share of challenges and failures and its triumphs and victories, Moses said that Abraham believed in God through it all: and Sarah tried really hard too!

Now, you may recall that in all of this great purpose the Lord had for them, there was one small, and almost insignificant, problem—Sarah was barren. She was physically unable to conceive and even have one child, much less give birth to a nation. I find it interesting that God, Abraham, or Sarah never addressed this small detail in their conversation.

Moses said in Gen.12:7 that the three of them, the Lord, Abraham, and Sarah, arrived at their destination, and this part of their adventure was over. As Abraham looked over the land, God promised him that He would give this land to his and Sarah's descendants forever. Still, however, the issue of barrenness remained unaddressed.

THE ILLUSION OF FAMINE

At this juncture, the barrenness of Sarah's womb was not the only obstacle they faced in the process of fulfilling their purpose. The Bible says that there was a grievous famine in the land. Can you imagine what Abraham must have been thinking—not even to mention Sarah's thoughts! As Abraham surveyed the countryside, he saw a land devoid of vegetation everywhere he looked: there was no water; therefore, there was no food source. He only saw a dry and thirsty land tightly held in the grip of a famine. Nothing Abraham could see was capable of sustaining their lives, much less a nation.

I'm not sure what your reaction might have been at this moment, but I think that if it had been me, I would have looked at the Lord and said something along the lines of "You know Lord, I appreciate it and all; it's nice and everything—but, do You think that maybe we took a wrong turn somewhere? Or maybe we missed a turn altogether?" I might have told Val, "Maybe His GPS wasn't recalculating and redirecting fast enough?" Not wanting to hurt the Lord's feelings or anything, I probably would have discretely leaned over to Val and whispered, "I'm not sure what's happened, because surely the Lord wouldn't have called us to this!"

I can picture Abraham giving the Lord a gratuitous ooohhh and a couple of aaahhh's: and then saying, "Okay, I think we've seen enough. Oh, don't get me wrong or anything, Lord…it's great and all, but maybe we can find somewhere a bit more…lively?"

God is a very methodical God. He never does anything without reason or purpose. This land was a picture, a reflection of Sarah's womb. It was barren and lifeless, and so was Sarah's womb. If you were to look at the same land about four hundred and fifty years later, when Abraham's descendants went to possess it, again like Sarah's womb, it was a fertile land that flowed with milk and honey. It was an abundantly fruitful land. You see, God never focuses on what is—He's focused on what will be. I have discovered that God is not as interested in what you were and what you've done as much as He is in what you become and do.

When the Lord showed the land to Abraham, all Abraham saw was famine along with all of the hardship's it produced. He saw a land that was parched, desolate, and formidable. That was the illusion! The Bible says in 1Sam.16:7 that the Lord does not see things as men see them. Men only focus on the surface of things. Abraham saw the illusion of what was, but God saw the reality of what it would become.

ATTENTION TO DETAILS

Allow me to fast-forward to Gen.15. In verse two, Abraham finally brings up the subject of Sarah's barrenness. He asked the Lord an honest question. Did you know that God is not afraid of your questions? You might be afraid to ask them, but He's never intimidated by our questions; on the contrary, He welcomes them, and can always provide an answer.

Abraham asked the Lord, "How?" How was He going to accomplish their purpose, seeing as how its fulfillment depended on Sarah and her barren womb? How would He give the land, the blessing, the promise to their seed when Sarah's womb had been shut? Abraham reasoned that God had made a promise concerning his descendants and that the closest thing he had to a son was his chief steward, Eliezer. Maybe the Lord was somehow going to use him? But he was a Syrian and not from his seed nor Sarah's womb.

In Gen.15:4, God declares a wonderfully prophetic word to Abraham, telling him that Eliezer would not be his heir but that an heir would come from him and Sarah. But the Lord wasn't finished yet. In my mind, I can see the Lord as He placed His arm around Abraham's shoulder and walked him out of his tent; the Lord then said to him, "Abraham, look now toward the heavens." In my mind, I can see Abraham as he lifted his eyes toward heaven and beheld millions of brilliant stars and galaxies. They all stood at attention, displaying all of their glory, knowing that their Creator was not only watching but using them as an example of His great and awesome power.

The Lord continued, "Abraham, if you can; if you are able, count the stars and tell Me their number." Abraham stood there speechless. He did not, would not have, could not have even known where or how to begin. Psalm 147:4 says that the Lord who called Abraham not only knew their number, but He also knew them all by name!

The Lord then finished His stellar object lesson by saying, "So will your descendants be." Then, Abraham does the craziest thing! Gen.15:6 says that he actually believed God, and God accredited it to him as righteousness.

Understand, at this point, that Abraham and Sarah had purpose as well as the presence: but as days passed into weeks, and weeks into months, and months into years—Sarah looked at her now well-aged and outdated body and that of Abraham's, and the promise seemed to her to now be even as they were—aged and outdated. It looked to Sarah to be an impossible situation. And the combination of time and circumstances caused Sarah to grow weary. In her weariness, she grew impatient with God. Her impatience clouded her judgment: and her clouded judgment caused her to make a decision that would temporarily cost her the very thing she needed to complete her purpose—the presence of the Lord.

Weariness produced impatience and the combination of the two blurred truth and confused thought. She began to rationalize that God needed some kind of assistance in fulfilling His promise; so she came up with a somewhat less than brilliant idea. She convinced Abraham to take Hagar, her Egyptian handmaid, to be his wife, and Abraham went in unto her. A seeming change in weather caused a fog to fill Sarah's mind, clouding her thoughts and restricting her vision. Instead of the promise being fulfilled in her, it would now somehow be fulfilled through Hagar. Crazy, huh? Weariness and impatience will cause a normally rational thinking person to think irrationally. Hagar indeed conceived, and she bore a son, and she called him Ishmael.

History has testified that at this point, although Abraham and Sarah still had purpose, they lacked the presence of God. And having only purpose, from the moment of Hagar's conception, things did not go well for them; there have been major issues and challenges between their generations, even unto this present day. And we are told from Scripture that these challenges will continue until the Lord returns and establishes His Kingdom upon the earth.

In Gen.17, four years after the birth of Ishmael, the Lord again appeared to Abraham. He identified Himself to Abraham as the Almighty God and admonished Abraham to walk before Him and be perfect—single in heart and committed to Him. God desired to connect Abraham and Sarah's purpose with His presence once again. Aren't you glad that the Lord doesn't give up on us!

He told Abraham to walk, converse, commune, and to foster fellowship with Him. This has always been God's greatest desire—that He would maintain fellowship with humanity and humanity with Him. And Abraham, in doing so, would be entire, complete, and whole. He would walk in truth, having no spot or blemish: he would be in the presence of God, undefiled and upright. This would reconnect purpose with presence.

In essence, God was telling Abraham that he should not have listened to Sarah in this matter, that he should have stayed on course and focused his attention on Him and His Word alone. We all know what it's like to be going through something and not quite see how we're going to get through it, much less see how we will come out of it alright on the other side. We've all had counselors like Sarah, who tell us what we should do and how we should do it. Although, like Sarah, they mean well, their counsel is counter-productive in reality.

It seems that it is when we are trying to figure out how the impossible can be made possible; if we are not careful, even the most unproductive, unwise, and consequential advice can seem the most credible: especially when we know our purpose. Still, in our thinking, there is a delay in its fulfillment. It is at this point that we are most likely to give birth to our own Ishmael.

We, as Christians, have purpose. We know that. Like Abraham and Sarah, God has called us to leave our family, our place of residency in this world, and follow Christ to the land, abundant with milk and honey, that He has promised us. And also, like Abraham and Sarah, we have been given exceeding great and precious promises. These prophetic words establish the purpose of God for our lives and the lives of others. But again, like Abraham and Sarah, we as Christians often give birth to our own Ishmael because purpose, unconnected to presence, drives us.

Like Abraham and Sarah, we have a word from the Lord, but we become weary and impatient in the process of fulfillment. We find ourselves unable or unwilling to wait in the presence of God and allow Him to release His glory on us, enabling us to complete our calling and election. We align ourselves with purpose only, and it becomes a bondwoman with whom we have relations that gives birth to a "son" that, just as Ishmael mocked and tormented Isaac, will mock our promise and seek to prevent its blessing for our lives. The result becomes disastrous, and the purpose, a burden.

Apostle Paul wrote in Gal.4:29 that just as the son born of purpose only persecuted the son born of the presence then, the same persecution remains even now. When we walk in purpose without presence, all that we produce comes from our will, intellect, talent, education, etc. And like Ishmael persecuted Isaac, what is birthed without the presence will persecute our promise.

By Gen.17, fifteen years had passed since the Lord first appeared to Abraham in Ur. Also, by this time, Abraham and Sarah had borne the burden of their choice for four years. They bore the strife, the contention, and the regret: all of which were consequences of choice. A good friend of mine once said that the power to choose is so great, the chooser will always serve their choice.

Think about choices that you have made over the course of your life. No doubt some of them have been good, and some not so good, and you wish that you could take them back and choose differently. However, wish as we might, choices made can never be taken back. We live with either the benefit or consequence of every choice we make in life. It's easy to serve the good choices, isn't it? It's those not-so-good choices that become so problematic. But we serve the good and the bad just the same. Why? Because the chooser always serves their choice. I say that if this is the case, and it is, we need to make sure we are choosing wisely.

Fortunately for us, Solomon wrote in Prov.1:20,21 that wisdom cries out: she speaks with her voice in the streets: she stands at the intersections and crossroads of life offering wise counsel to those to whom she calls. Solomon said basically the same thing again in Prov.8:1-3. I think that maybe wisdom is trying to get our attention before we pass through an intersection, helping us to stay on the right road that will lead us to our destiny in Christ.

Godly wisdom is never hidden, nor is it silent. If wisdom seems silent to us, it's because we are not looking for her or listening for her voice. Wisdom constantly seeks to turn our attention away from foolish counselors and their foolish counsel: and to speak to us concerning things that belong to godly knowledge and understanding.

GOD'S GRACE STILL AMAZES ME

One of the things I find amazing about God is His truly amazing grace; and His desire to see us succeed. It was in the middle of Abraham's failure that the Lord appeared to him to encourage him and to reconnect His presence with Abraham's purpose.

God again expressed His intention to abundantly multiply Abraham and Sarah. In Gen.17:6, the Lord said that they would be fruitful, producing nations and kingdoms. In Gen.17:16, the Lord said concerning Sarah that He would bless her and that He would give them a son through her and that she would be the mother of nations and kings.

DELAYED FOR HIS GLORY

Have you ever wondered why the Lord waited twenty-five years to fulfill His promise made to Abraham and Sarah? I am confident that the Lord could have caused Sarah's womb to conceive in the morning, and she could have birthed Isaac before lunch! Why the wait? Why twenty-five years later?

I think that there are two very good reasons. First, so that when it happened, everyone would know that God did it. In Abraham's day, people aged very differently than they do now. When God first came to Abraham, he was seventy-five years old, and Sarah was sixty-five. Because of the variation in the aging process of their time, it was conceivable that Abraham and Sarah could still conceive and birth children. If Sarah had conceived at the time of the promise, it could have been argued that she, through nature, luck, or chance, conceived, and then one of these lesser things could have been credited instead of God. Waiting twenty-five years knocked the props out from under natural means, and all eyes would have been focused on the Lord's power, resulting in Him alone receiving the glory.

The second reason I think that there was a delay is that Abraham had an exceeding great and precious promise from God, and he had to come to a place where he was willing to sacrifice the promise out of his love for God and his relationship with God. The Lord will allow nothing, not even a promise He's given, to stand between He and us. In this twenty-five-year journey, Abraham grew close to God. He trusted Him. He believed Him and became His friend.

He came to a place in his relationship with God where he found himself willing to sacrifice his promise if it stood between him and God—and he also knew that had the promise been sacrificed, God was able to raise it and restore it back to him.

God, too, has given us exceedingly great and precious promises. Some are corporate promises, and we receive some promises on a more personal and intimate level. But, as in the case of Abraham, these wonderful promises of God cannot stand between God and us. We cannot focus on the gift more than the giver. We must love God more than the promise He gave us. If this is not established, we can find ourselves loving the promise more than the God who gave it.

Many of us are captivated by the hand of God instead of being captivated by His face. I often say that the devil has taken away the fishing rods that Jesus gave the Church and replaced them with butterfly nets, and he keeps us busy running through the meadows of promise, trying to catch the butterflies of blessings instead of fishing the seas of humanity for the souls of men.

CONGRATULATIONS! IT'S A BOY!!

Val and I have four sons, and although they are all grown, I can still remember when each one of them was born. I remember how even though we had nine months to plan and prepare for each of them, it seemed that we were never ready for the big day! Even when we knew the time for the delivery was close, it always seemed to me that suddenly and from out of nowhere, Val would say, "it's time!" And we would still have nothing prepared. We would throw a bunch of useless things in a bag, rush out to the car, where I would stuff her ever so gently in, and then drive to the hospital like a madman. Each time we would barely get inside the hospital and to a room before I would hear the doctor say, "Geeze, that was quick!" Then, almost in the same breath he would say, "Congratulations! It's a boy!" Four times this exact same scenario would play itself out. I literally could have recorded the doctor's words the first time and replayed them three more times.

Abraham and Sarah had made a monumental mistake in getting ahead of God and moving forward in their purpose without His presence. But from it, they learned a valuable lesson. They learned to wait on God.

They learned first hand the value of Solomon's words in Prov.10:22 when he said that the blessing of the Lord makes rich, and He adds no sorrow with it. Surely, they had known their share of sorrow, the consequence of choices made. Eliezer was not to be their blessing, and neither was Ishmael: Isaac was. And it didn't take long for this to become very, very apparent.

Gen.17 tells us that when their purpose was once again connected to the Lord's presence, even though their journey from promise to possession continued for ten more years, they were determined to not repeat the same mistakes of the past. This time, they were determined to wait on the Lord.

By Gen.21, Abraham had reached his one-hundredth birthday, and Sarah, her ninetieth. But that was not the big news. No! The big news was that their time had come, and their wait was over. This was to be the year of blessing and increase. It was to be the time when presence and purpose would come together and become one. This was their big day: the day they waited twenty-five long years for. This was the day both their dreams and nightmares were about. Gen.21:1 says that the Lord "visited" Sarah. The word "visited" means that He remembered Sarah and went to pay her a visit. It was in this time of visitation that, at the age of ninety, God reconstructed Sarah's womb making her able to conceive.

I can picture Sarah as she looked at Abraham with that look in her eye. And Abraham went over to the shelf and blew the dust from a Barry White album that had long since been put away. Abraham placed the record on the turntable and, nine months later, Sarah gave birth to a son whom they called Isaac.

AS ABRAHAM WAS...SO ARE WE

By possessing the same faith that was in Abraham, we are the children of Abraham. As Abraham was...so are we. As I said earlier, like God called Abraham out from among his family and his country, we are called by God, at the point of salvation, to come out from among the world and its system. The Apostle Paul said in Ehp.2 that at one time, we were all dead in trespass and sin. We were controlled by the prince and power of the air, who is the spirit of bondage that works bondage in the children of disobedience.

God called Abraham out of Ur. The people who lived in Ur were idolaters. According to Josh.24:2, even Abraham was an idolater before God's presence connected with his purpose. The people who lived in Ur were dead as a result of their trespass and sin—Paul said we were too. In reality, Ur was not a city but a graveyard full of tombs that housed dead men and women, and it reeked of death and decay. In this way, Ur was a type of the world: a place filled with idolaters. Ur was a habitation of the dead. And the same could be said of our world today. Abraham was a type of the Church, and the calling of Abraham out of Ur was prophetically a symbol of God calling the Church of Jesus Christ out of the world. And like God sent Abraham on a journey to possess a promise, He has sent the Church on a journey for the same.

In this, we are a type of Abraham: we represent him. If the Church represents Abraham, then Sarah would represent faith. Abraham and Sarah were both needed to conceive, develop, birth, and possess the promise—Isaac. Just like Abraham + Sarah = Isaac, the Church + faith = the promise. We must have a relationship with faith. In a sense, we must be married to her in order for our purpose to connect with presence and produce the promise.

But it is here where a problem can occur. Purpose without presence becomes a type of bondwoman that produces a substitute son but cannot produce the son of promise. God gives to us a promise, a purpose which is what we have been called to do. And instead of waiting on God and going in unto Sarah, who represents faith, we go in unto Hagar, which represents the bondwoman of purpose without presence.

The bondwoman represents any other way we use to fulfill the promise God gave to us. She represents anything or anyone that we involve ourselves with or have relationship with that is not contained within the presence of God. Because Sarah represents faith, she also represents the presence; because in order for us to have the presence, we must have faith. Isaac represents the promise. The bondwoman represents a substitution for the presence resulting in the birth of an Ishmael—who was a substitute for the promise.

God has a tremendous plan and purpose for our lives, but if we are not patient and focused on the plan, we can substitute faith and become involved with a bondwoman. We end up, like Abraham, marrying multiple wives and having multiple problems. We end up with polar opposite "wives" who are enemies.

God is a God of covenant. It was God's covenant with Abraham that forced Him to make a great nation from Hagar and Ishmael: because the promise was to Abraham and his seed, of which Ishmael was. When we get impatient and marry the bondwoman, a grievous and burdensome son is born because we are in the same covenant as Abraham. The same terminology used to describe Isaac was used to describe Ishmael. God said that Ishmael would have purpose; but his covenant, His presence, would be with Isaac. This is why Israel will never be moved.

You have to know that when God heard the sound of Abraham and Hagar's wedding bells, it caught His attention, and although He wasn't invited, He showed up at the wedding! Also, I do not think He was too happy about it all. But for His grace…

Just like Abraham went in unto Hagar in the sight of Sarah, we go into the bondwoman in the sight of faith. And when the bondwoman conceives, and gives birth, just like Sarah hated Hagar and Hagar hated Sarah, the bondwoman will hate faith, and faith will hate the bondwoman. They cannot and will not cohabitate. One is sacrificed for the other.

And not only does the bondwoman of purpose without presence despise faith, the son she births will mock faith and mock the promise: both will hate you and ultimately seek to destroy you.

The Lord said concerning Ishmael that he would be a wild man. This means that he would run like a donkey, kicking and biting at everyone and everything. He said that Ishmael's hand would be against every man and every man's hand against him. Finally, the Lord said that the descendants of Ishmael would cause trouble for the descendants of Isaac throughout history.

Don't be mistaken, beloved. Just as sure as the descendants of Ishmael have frustrated, hated, and fought against the descendants of Isaac; biting and kicking at them as the Lord said they would: if we move forward in our purpose without the presence, there will come a time when what is birthed by the bondwoman of our impatience will become a grievous burden to us. And the grief they cause will end up affecting generations to come. We will reap the fruit of what we sow.

Without the presence, Abraham had sown to the wind, and he reaped a whirlwind. But when purpose reconnected with presence, it produced the promise that has truly been a blessing to all the families of the earth. When presence reconnects with purpose, it will cast out the bondwoman—and her son.

Chapter Three

――――――⧲――――――

From Deceiver to Prince

THE HUNTER AND THE MAMA'S BOY

JACOB WAS A MAN WITH a purpose, but he was a man without the presence when he and his mother plotted against his brother, Esau, to steal the birthright blessing. According to Gen.25:23, his purpose was to be the progenitor of a nation: more specifically, the nation of Israel. More than likely, you already know that Jacob's name means deceiver or supplanter. The Biblical definition of "supplanter" is one who wrongfully or illegally seizes and holds the place of another. Certainly, this would describe Jacob.

Gen.25:27 says that as Esau grew, he became a mighty man of the field: he was a country boy that loved to hike. He enjoyed camping and sleeping out under the stars. He liked to get his hands dirty. But he especially loved to hunt. Esau loved to track various kinds of game and then experience the thrill of the chase. He, like Cain, was a man's man. He loved the earth, and he smelled like it. He was strong and rugged, and his father, Isaac, loved him.

But on the other hand, the Bible says that Jacob was a "plain" man. The word "plain" from Hebrew means that Jacob was a clean man. Unlike his brother, Esau, Jacob was a man that didn't like getting dirty. He didn't like getting dirt under his fingernails. He was a soft and gentle man. Jacob and Esau could not have been any more opposite of each other. Jacob was not a hiker, camper, or hunter. He was a tent dweller, and he enjoyed the creature comforts that the "tent" afforded to him. He enjoyed the domestic life. He was the type that, if possible, would like to have had his own cooking show and probably would have called it something like "Cooking with Jake."

He was an insecure man to a degree, and he also was a manipulative man. All of these things lead me to believe that those who knew Jacob thought him to be sort of, if not entirely, a mama's boy. He was everything that Esau wasn't, and his mama loved him.

As I said in the previous chapter, Val and I have four sons. They grew up in a small town in a very rural part of Northeast Nevada, and they love the outdoors. They love hiking, camping, fishing, and especially hunting. It probably comes as no surprise that none of them like to shop unless they are going to an outdoor store that can equip the outdoorsman with every outdoor thing imaginable.

Two of our sons, like Esau, are avid hunters. Usually, they'll go out in the mountains and not come home until one of two things happens: they either bag their trophy deer, or their time is over, and they have to go back to work.

At times, there have been conflicts in work schedules that wouldn't allow them to hunt together, so, from time to time, it would fall on me to accompany them on their hunt. I have a confession to make to you: I'm not really an outdoorsy kind of guy. I'm sort of like Jacob in this. I grew up in the city. My idea of a good hunting trip is to stalk the meat case at our local market until I spot my cut and pre-wrapped trophy beef and then place it in a plastic bag, so I don't get cow blood on my hands. My idea of a good fishing trip is a visit to the seafood case. And my idea of farming is the produce department. I don't like to camp; I don't like insects. I don't like not being able to shower—you get the picture. Like Jacob, I'm kind of a clean, soft, and gentle man. And although I don't consider myself to be a mama's boy, my sons would probably tell you that I am. But then again, Jacob probably didn't consider himself one either.

THE SOUP COSTS HOW MUCH?

One day, Esau returned home from a rather unsuccessful hunting trip. He was very hot, very tired, and very hungry. As he drew closer to home, he could smell the wonderful aroma of lentil soup. As its fragrance was wafting gently up into the air; a light breeze carried it right in Esau's direction. Sure enough, there was Jacob wearing his "kiss the cook" apron, and there on the fire next to him was a fresh, hot kettle of soup that he had just finished cooking. With renewed determination, Esau summoned every ounce of strength that he could muster, and he made his way over to Jacob and his signature, life-saving lentil soup.

Crawling toward Jacob like he had just come out of Death Valley in the summer, having gone days without food or water, Esau (who at the time had a flare for the dramatic), with his dry and parched mouth, whispered to Jacob, "Brother, for the love of God, I beg you, feed me! Please let me have some of your soup, or I, I shall die…"
(Gen.25:30 paraphrased).

Now, Jacob had purpose without presence as he watched Esau's Academy Award-winning performance (or maybe he watched it because he was a deceiver and a manipulator) without sympathy.

He said to Esau, "I'll give you some of my soup, and in exchange, I want something from you." Nobody ate Jacob's lentil soup for free, especially Esau.

Jacob dipped his spoon into the soup and stirred it slowly. Each time it went around the pot, Esau's eyes followed it undistracted. Jacob pulled out a large portion of soup with his ladle and then, allowed it to flow like a delicious and savory waterfall back into the pot. He poured a spoonful slowly into a bowl, with Esau's eyes fastened on the soup that was now filling the bowl. Finally, Jacob said to him, "I'll feed you, but it's going to cost you. I won't give it to you, but I will sell it. For a price, Esau, you can have this big, delicious bowl of my soup." Jacob then said, "I'll give you this soup, and you give me your birthright."

The birthright went to the firstborn, and the reason Jacob wanted the birthright was because with it came the privileges of the firstborn, which included the majority of the inheritance and the highest place of position and honor in the family. The one with the birthright was like the godfather. And after Jacob made Esau an offer that he couldn't refuse, Esau sold his birthright to Jacob for an exceptionally cheap meal.

The Bible says that Esau ate and drank, then went his way. The final sentence of Gen.25:34 reads like an epithet over the life of Esau that would eternally define him, "Thus Esau despised his birthright." Jacob now had purpose, and he had the birthright, but what he really needed and didn't have, was the presence.

A PLOT THICKER THAN SOUP

As the world turns, we get older. Isaac, Jacob and Esau's father, was no exception. The Bible says in Gen.27, that Isaac's eye sight was all but gone, and he now "saw" with his hands and his sense of smell rather than with his eyes. Isaac's eyes were dim, and his body worn out, but his mind was sharp. For him to stand and release the blessing would require someone to assist him and then hold him steady in that position. He relied on the assistance of a cane and would probably have loved a power chair. Isaac knew that the time for him to go the way of all the earth was drawing near.

But before he could make the journey to the bosom of his father, Abraham, he had one last thing to do. He held one more thing in his hands.

I often tell the Lord that I don't want to leave this earth one minute before my hands are empty, and I don't want to stay here one minute after they are—and neither did Isaac. The last thing Isaac held in his hands was the blessing of the birthright. In Isaac's day, blessings were powerful. They had the power to define, shape, and determine destiny.

It is clear from Gen.27 that Isaac had never known about the meeting between Jacob and Esau. He was unaware that Esau had sold his birthright to Jacob. Somehow, he never got the memo.

Isaac called his son, his boy, Esau. The man's man; the hunter: the earthy-smelling man. He called the boy he loved, and Esau came to him. Isaac was ready to conduct his final act as a father and prophet. He was ready to release the blessing of the birthright. But Isaac was hungry, and before he could give the blessing, he had to eat. He had an appetite all set for some fresh venison. So, he sent Esau, the hunter, out to hunt for deer.

By this time, I believe that Esau had forgotten all about the whole selling of his birthright thing to Jacob. He went on living his life without the thought of the cost or consequence of his decision. Esau may have forgotten, but Jacob didn't. Jacob was shrewd. He had gotten the birthright. In his mind, he not only wanted the blessing, but he also he needed it. Because he had purpose without presence, his purpose drove him to have Isaac's blessing. He reasoned that if he had the blessing of his father, he would be able to fulfill his purpose of being a great nation.

Now, it would seem that Rebekah had to have been made aware of what Jacob had done. That's what mama's boy's do; they tell their moms things. While Esau was out hunting, Rebekah concocted a plan: a plan that would not only give Jacob the birthright, but the blessing as well. Moms can be so sneaky! She instructed Jacob to go to the goat pen and get one of the young goats. She told him that she would prepare the meal for Isaac while Esau was gone; and that when it was ready, Jacob would take it into Isaac's tent. After Isaac had eaten and enjoyed the meal, he would surely place the prophetic blessing on Jacob.

One problem stood between them and success, however. There was the issue of Jacob being clean, soft, and gentle. Even with his poor eyesight, Isaac would see right through this charade. He would readily know that the one who came in for the blessing was "his mother's son." The result would certainly be a curse instead of a blessing placed on Jacob by Isaac for being a deceiver.

Rebekah's plan was to glue animal hair on Jacob; after all, they were twins...sort of. And then Isaac would be none the wiser. So, Rebekah glued animal hair on Jacob and, for good measure, had him roll around in the dirt so that he would lose his clean scent and take on a more earthy, musky, no shower for a week's smell.

If you're familiar with the story, you'll know that Jacob took the meal towards Isaac, and he savored every bite. I am confident that Jacob was a very scared boy during that meal. He was afraid of what would happen if his father, the promise of Abraham, the prophetic speaker, found out that his younger son was deceiving him; because although his younger son possessed the purpose of God for his life, it had not yet been connected with the presence of God.

One of the great problems with telling lies is that you can't just tell one. Once you've told a lie, then there usually comes another lie to try and cover the first one. After that, there are so many inconsistencies that the original lie becomes totally unbelievable and unrealistic. When Jacob spoke, his father recognized the voice. As the father of four, when one of my sons calls me on the phone, I know exactly which one of the four the voice belongs to. Isaac knew the voice, even though he couldn't see the man. Isaac must have sensed that there was something that was not quite right. He began to interrogate Jacob. He then called him over to him for a closer inspection. First, Isaac felt Jacob's arms and neck. Then he smelled Jacob, who smelled like earth, among other things. Satisfied with the results, while Esau was chasing deer, Jacob was chasing the blessing, and Jacob caught his before Esau caught his: and Isaac began to prophetically release the blessing of the first born on Jacob.

A BLESSING AND A ONE-WAY TICKET

The blessing that Isaac spoke over Jacob reached the heights of heaven and spread over the face of the whole earth, including every nation and kingdom. And it was about to reach the ears of Esau.

As you can imagine, when Esau found out that Jacob had received the first-born blessing, he was somewhat less than happy. In fact, it caused him to go into an uncontrollable rage. When Isaac found out what happened, he trembled, meaning that he was shaken to the core because of the power, position, and prosperity of the blessing given to Jacob, that by custom, should have gone to Esau—and would have had not God intervened on behalf of Jacob's purpose.

Looking into the future, God saw a time where Jacob's purpose would connect with His presence, and through divine providence, He steered Jacob toward a course that would cause his purpose to collide with His presence.

Purpose without presence caused Jacob to flee for his life. In Esau's anger and bitterness of soul, only one thing would satisfy him...revenge. I always say that revenge is a dish best served by God.

Esau wanted to kill Jacob. Purpose without presence caused Jacob to have to purchase a one-way ticket to Padan-aram, and for the next twenty years, Jacob would call it home.

It was here that Jacob met his mother's brother, Laban, and his family. As it turns out, Jacob and Laban had more in common than blood. It wouldn't be long before Jacob discovered that Laban was a deceiver like himself. For twenty years, Laban gave Jacob tablespoons of his own medicine, and for the first time, Jacob realized just how unpleasant it was to swallow.

It was during this time that God began to manifest glimpses of His presence as it moved closer toward Jacob's life. Like a small shaft of light piercing through the ominous storm clouds that followed Jacob: the presence began to break through the darkness that accompanied his purpose without the Lord's presence. It is here that God began to bless, increase, and position Jacob.

·OVERCOMING THE FEARS OF THE PAST

There came a point in Padan-aram that Jacob began to feel the winds of change blowing once again, and he felt in his heart that it was time for him to return home: to the place where his mother was and to where his father had blessed him. But also, he would be returning to the place where his brother was.

You'll recall that when Jacob left twenty years earlier, they were not on the best of terms. For Jacob, it was like yesterday.

Thoughts of uncertainty filled his mind. Old fears rose up within him. While on the journey home, Jacob had heard that Esau was coming in his direction, and he became very afraid. I often say that fear, real or imagined, has the same effect. He divided his family into two groups thinking that if Esau was still angry with him and still seeking revenge, at least half of his family would be safe. Jacob sent wave after wave of servants to Esau, who brought gifts to him in hopes that he would forgive him and spare him and his family.

Jacob was flat-out scared at the thought of encountering Esau. The Bible says in Gen.32:7 that Jacob was "greatly distressed." The word distress means to feel like you are emotionally and mentally being pulled apart, to the point where it begins to take a physical toll as well.

The shaft of presence began to widen a little bit more in Gen.32:9 when Jacob called out to the Lord saying, "Lord, you were the One who told me to return to my home, and that You would deal well with me." Jacob had repented of his deceptive and manipulative manner. He acknowledged his unworthiness of the Lord's mercies: but he pleaded with Him to be merciful and deliver his family from what he thought would be a wrathful, vengeful Esau. He reminded God of what He said would take place when great purpose would connect with a greater presence. Purpose had gotten Jacob the birthright and Isaac's blessing, but he still lacked the presence: and it caused him to spend years running from the past and its fears.

IN THE OCTAGON WITH GOD

After sending many gifts to Esau and dividing his family into groups and sending them on ahead, the Bible says in Gen.32:24 that Jacob was left alone...but he was not alone.

That night, Jacob went from being purpose driven to presence driven, when the Lord happened upon him. The Bible is not very clear on the sequence of events that led to Jacob wrestling the Lord. What we do know is that as Jacob sat, a man came to him and engaged him in conversation. No doubt this man, who was the Lord, began to speak to Jacob, and as He spoke, Jacob's heart burned. I am reminded of Jesus after His resurrection who joined Himself to two of His disciples while they walked toward Emmaus. As Jesus spoke to them, their hearts began to burn within them. These disciples wouldn't let Jesus go.

They pleaded with Him to come home with them; they listened intently to every word Jesus spoke. I can imagine that here on this night, the same sort of scenario was playing itself out. As the Lord spoke to Jacob, even though He did not reveal Himself to him, Jacob knew there was more to this man than just a passerby. I think that as the Lord rose and made like He would leave; Jacob grabbed him and didn't let Him go. One thing led to another, and the match was on.

The Lord and Jacob wrestled throughout the night and unto the rising of the sun. I cannot quite imagine this. When I was in high school, I took boxing. We went through three rounds. Back then, I thought I was in pretty good shape; but after two full rounds, I got to where I couldn't even lift my hands, my arms up. No matter how hard I tried or willed my hands to raise, they would not: and I was left with no alternative but to fling my arms wildly from side to side and hope that I hit my opponent before they hit me. I can't imagine wrestling through the night. But Jacob was determined. He knew that this man was special and that He had the power to bless him, and he would indeed be blessed. Jacob would tell his opponent that he would not let Him go until He placed a blessing on him. Even when the Lord touched his leg and knocked Jacob's hip out of joint, he held onto Him for dear life! He refused to let go. Although they were written several hundred years later, Jacob understood the words of Jesus recorded in Matt.11:12 when He said, "The Kingdom of heaven suffers violence, and the violent take it by force." Jacob was determined; he had made up his mind that he was not letting the Lord go until He blessed him, until He connected His presence with Jacob's purpose.

Jacob had gone too long only having purpose. He was done being only driven by purpose. He had gotten an attitude and grabbed hold of some moxie. On this night, he would go from being purpose driven to being presence driven!

It's amazing to me what desperation will do to a man. Desperation is a powerful force. Desperation will cause a man to do things that they normally would never have thought of doing. Jacob was a desperate man: desperate for the presence. His desperation caused him to put the Lord in a full nelson and not give up, in, or out, until the presence of God came together with the purpose of Jacob, and the two became one.

THE ROYAL DECREE

The Lord said to Jacob, "your name shall (a statement of fact) no longer be called Jacob (deceiver) but Israel." The name Israel means to prevail as a prince and to rule as a prince with God. If you stop and think about it, before we were born again, we all had purpose, and we were all like Jacob. We were all deceivers and spent our time deceiving and being deceived. We all were trying to steal our way to obtain the birthright and the blessing, although we didn't realize it. But when we were born again, and our purpose connected to His presence, we went from being a deceiver to princes…ruling as a Kingdom of priests with our God and His Christ.

Jacob walked into this encounter with the presence of a deceiver and came out with a new identity. He went in with weakness and came out with power and strength. He went into this encounter with the presence with fear and came out with confidence. He went in with shame and came out with honor. When Jacob's purpose was infused with God's presence, he found that there was peace, forgiveness, and favor that came with it.

Jacob would indeed meet Esau later that day. All of the fear, anxiety, and uncertainty that he carried for the last twenty years was gone when Esau saw Jacob and came running to him and embraced him. They wept tears of relief, forgiveness, reconciliation, and joy. That day Jacob, the deceiver, died, and Israel, the prince of God, emerged. In essence, when Jacob's purpose connected with the Lord's presence, a nation was born and it was as if Jacob had been born again.

Chapter Four

⌁

The Prince, the Fugitive, and the Deliverer

THE PRINCE

IF THERE EVER WAS A man that had purpose, Moses would have been that man. Moses' purpose was to deliver Israel from Egyptian bondage and to lead them into the land that God had promised Abraham to give to his seed as an inheritance. Scripture tells us that beginning with Jacob's son, Joseph, and continuing into the events leading to Israel's exodus, God blessed, multiplied, and increased Israel abundantly. They became a strong nation within a nation, and they began to fill the land of Egypt.

Scripture also tells us that several hundred years had come and gone since days of Joseph and that a new Pharaoh who didn't know (or care) about Joseph was in town now. All of the contributions that Joseph had made had long since been forgotten in Egypt. This often seems to be the way of life, doesn't it? Most of the time, no matter how significant the contributions are that were made, or by whom they were made, they have a tendency to simply fade away into obscurity over time.

The Pharaoh and the Egyptian people may have forgotten all that Joseph did for their nation: they might have forgotten how he advised them during the years of famine—but the God of heaven had not. But then, He never forgets anything. The Bible says in Heb.6:10 that God will never forget the work that we do in His name and for His glory. He remembers and rewards us accordingly. We can be sure of that.

The Bible makes it very clear that God's blessing was on Israel. And it was this very blessing, a blessing that released prosperity in His people, that increased the internal fears and insecurities in the Pharaoh and throughout Egypt. Why? Because the blessing of the righteous is the curse of the wicked! The Pharaoh viewed Israel as a very real and formidable threat to his empire and to the Egyptian people. However, the real threat was not Israel; the real threat was Israel's God!

The Pharaoh believed that he needed to come up with a plan that would prevent an Israeli uprising. He came up with a plan that was two-fold. First, he set out to demoralize them. To accomplish this, he took away their rights, property, and possessions. He afflicted them, oppressed them, and enslaved them. We would be wise to understand that slavery is not a color; it's a condition. But if we can assign a color to it, then we can keep those of the assigned color oppressed and instill in them the victim's mentality, assuring they will always be oppressed and, in a way, accepting of it. I am of the opinion that a man who truly understands and appreciates freedom will never seek to enslave another man.

The Pharaoh set taskmasters over the people of God. A taskmaster was someone who was positioned as a ruler, lording over the people. Taskmasters forced the Israelites to labor in building cities and heavily oppressed them in the process. They were often humiliated and beaten in order to break their will and bring them into submission. The Pharaoh wanted to take their dignity and destroy their purpose and destiny. This strategy should sound familiar to us. If we look around our world today, it is much the same strategy that Satan uses to demoralize, oppress, and beat humanity into submission to his will. Thanks be to God, who just as he sent Moses to deliver Israel and bring them into their promise, He sent Jesus to deliver us and bring us into our promise.

The second part of the Pharaoh's plan was to kill all the male Hebrew children. He decreed that all males born to Hebrew women were to be thrown into the river and drowned upon birth. It was under these conditions that the Bible says in Ex.2:2 that Moses was born.

According to verse two, Moses was a goodly child: meaning that he was a handsome and pleasant boy. Moses' mother did the best she could to hide him for three months, but she found that she could no longer keep him a secret. Being unable to just cast her son into the river, and hoping against hope, she made a basket and placed Moses in it, believing that God would somehow intervene on her behalf and rescue Moses alive.

After she placed Moses in the water, her heart broken, she turned and walked away. She was unable to watch the basket as it began to be carried by the river current: but her daughter, Merriam, stayed behind. She believed that somehow, someway, this would not be the last memories that she would have of her baby brother.

Indeed, the Pharaoh had a plan…but so did God. The Pharaoh's plan was much like what Jesus said Satan's plan was in John 10:10=to steal, kill, and destroy. But God's plan was to rescue, redeem, restore, and plant His covenant people in their promise. King David wrote in Psalm 33:10-11, "The Lord brings the plans of the wicked to nothing: He makes the intentions of the people of no effect. The plans of the Lord will stand forever, the thoughts of His heart to all generations." Solomon wrote in Prov.19:21 "There are many plans in a man's heart; nevertheless, the plans of the Lord will stand." God had a plan for Israel and purpose for Moses, a great purpose.

Although Moses' mother could not see it, God had His hand on that basket, on its contents, on Moses. She couldn't have imagined that when she released Moses into the river that day, she released him into the hand of God, who from before his birth had ordained his purpose. When her hand let go of the basket, God's unseen hand gently reached out and took control of its movement. He guided the basket that held Moses toward a part of the river's bank where He anchored it in some tall reeds that grew along the river's edge: and there it remained until this future rescuer could himself be rescued.

As divine providence would have it, about that same time, the Pharaoh's daughter came down to the river to bathe. As she walked along the bank, with her attendants looking for the perfect spot for her to refresh herself, she heard the pitiful cry of a baby. She spotted the basket and sent one of her maids to retrieve it. When she opened it, there was Moses, frightened, weeping, helpless, beautiful, and no doubt in need of a diaper change.

Talk about a divine appointment! From that moment, the Pharaoh's daughter took Moses as her own and raised him in the palace. Moses' sister had witnessed the whole thing! She was still watching over Moses as all of this unfolded. When the Pharaoh's daughter took Moses, Miriam asked her if she wanted her to find a Hebrew woman to nurse Moses. She agreed, and again through divine providence, Moses' mother became his nurse. It would be just as the Lord had planned it; the one who was delivered would be raised by his own mother and become the one whose purpose was to deliver.

At this time, Egypt was one of the world's greatest and most advanced civilizations. No doubt Moses was being educated by the finest Egyptian scholars and educators, who instructed him in the sciences, arts, and literature.

He was taught royal protocol and etiquette. He was being groomed as a prince and potential heir to the throne. Moses surely had purpose from birth…but just as surely as he had purpose, he lacked presence.

From early on, Moses knew that he was not like other Egyptian boys. I am confident that as his mother nursed him, she told him about how she defied the Pharaoh's decree as long as she could: and how she made a basket, placed him in it, and trusted God would somehow save him. No doubt, she instilled his Hebrew heritage in him as she spoke. O, how his purpose must have burned within him as he listened.

In Exodus Ch.2, we see that Moses had purpose without presence when he went out to check on his Hebrew brethren. He saw an Egyptian beating a Hebrew. Moses' purpose caused him to follow the Egyptian until they had come to a secluded place. In Moses' thinking, he had followed the Egyptian who led him to the perfect place to exact revenge. The Bible said that Moses looked up and down the street, and not seeing anyone, he slew the Egyptian.

Feeling good about his purpose as a deliverer, the very next day, Moses set out again to check on his brethren. This time, however, he encountered two of his own fighting with each other in the street. Our would-be superhero stopped his chariot and, stepping out of it, went over to the two men. He asked the one who had started the fight why he hit his brother. The man replied to Moses, "Who made you a prince and a judge over us? Are you going to kill me like you did that Egyptian?"

Indeed, Moses was a prince and a judge, but because he had purpose without presence, this man did not recognize nor did he honor Moses' purpose or position. Purpose without presence caused fear to grip Moses' heart. He speculated that his killing of the Egyptian was a known matter: and he was correct. The Pharaoh indeed knew that Moses had killed an Egyptian to save the life of a Hebrew. His only option now was to run… fast, furiously, and…far.

THE FUGITIVE

Purpose without presence took Moses from prince to fugitive. Exodus 2:15 says that Moses ran until he came to the land of Midian. He found a well and sat by it to rest.

Verse 16 says that the daughters of the priest of Midian, whose name was Jethro, came to the well to water their sheep.

After they had filled the troughs with water, a group of shepherds came and forced them and their flocks to leave, and then they began to water their own. Moses took offense to this. His purpose as a deliverer would not allow him to sit idly by and do nothing about this great injustice. Once again, Moses the super hero sprang into action and came to their defense. And, having driven these shepherds and their flocks away, Moses watered Jethro's daughter's sheep. It was here at this well that Moses met Zipporah, the daughter of Jethro, that would soon become his wife.

The reason I bring this up is because of how she described Moses to her father. Exodus 2:19 says that as Zipporah was relating the story to her father of how Moses rescued them and their flocks to her father, she described

Moses as an Egyptian. The problem was that Moses was not an Egyptian; he was a Hebrew. Here's my point. Purpose without presence caused Moses to lose his identity. He was a deliverer; he was a Hebrew. He was a descendent of Abraham, Isaac, and Jacob. But in having purpose only, he was incorrectly defined, misunderstood, and wrongly identified as an Egyptian. When we as the Church have purpose without the presence, our purpose can also be indefinable, misunderstood, and wrongly identified.

Purpose without presence caused Moses to run for his life, and he didn't stop running until he found himself on the backside of the desert, tending a few sheep that didn't even belong to him. Purpose without presence can move you out of position and send you on a journey that can prevent, or at least delay, what you've been anointed and called to do. It can hinder your destiny and has the potential of making your life inconsequential. It can have you tending a handful of sheep instead of delivering nations.

Think about this for a moment. What might it have been like for Moses, for Israel, for Egypt if Moses had waited until his purpose was connected to God's presence? What if Moses had become the next Pharaoh? What if? Could it be possible that so much of what happened with Moses after he fled Egypt—his challenges to the Pharaoh, the exodus, Israel's wilderness years, the plagues, the rebellions, the battles Israel fought might have never occurred? How different might it have been if Moses had waited on the presence of God to connect with his purpose? Certainly, this side of heaven, we will never know.

Even here, in this desolate place, the presence followed Moses. I find it fascinating that even through our mistakes, failures, foolishness, misdirection, impatience, etc., God still is able to direct our path so that His presence will intercept our purpose, and we are still able to complete our calling and election in Christ.

CONNECTING PURPOSE WITH PRESENCE

After almost eighty years, Moses finally went from purpose to presence with purpose one day as he was in the wilderness tending Jethro's sheep.

Moses' journey led him to the place where presence had been waiting to intercept his purpose.

Ex.3:2 says that the Lord appeared to Moses in a most unique way. He appeared to him in the form of a raging fire. As Moses moved the flock, he looked up and saw in the distance that a bramble bush was engulfed in a flame; but it had not ignited. Bramble bushes can grow quite large. Many have thorns on them: and some produce various kinds of edible berries. This miraculous wonder captivated Moses' attention. He decided that he needed to take a closer look.

THE POWER OF CURIOSITY

Curiosity is a powerful force. They say that curiosity killed the cat—but it also can catapult the curious to their destiny. What if Moses hadn't been curious? What if he had seen the bush, but decided that he didn't want to get involved? What if he just glanced at it and then kept on walking? There are several examples of people whose encounter with Jesus was birthed out of curiosity. Might I encourage us to stay curious!

We know that there are people who talk to themselves, don't we? More than likely, you know people who talk to themselves. Maybe you talk to yourself. I will admit to you that I talk to myself probably more frequently than I should. But have you ever wondered if people like Moses ever talked to themselves? Wonder no longer! Ex.3:3 says that Moses (who wrote the Book of Exodus; and, talking to himself, said) "I will turn aside, and see this great sight, why the bush is not burnt." Those of us who talk to ourselves really needn't worry; we're in some very good company. Even Jesus talked to Himself. Sometimes you have to talk to yourself so that you can take control of your thoughts and emotions and set them in order. And there are those times that we talk to ourselves because we're the only ones that will listen to us!

As Moses cautiously walked toward the bush, the Lord spoke to him from within the bush and told him to take off his shoes because the ground he was standing on was holy ground: but the ground, in and of itself, was not holy. In our world, there are religions that classify certain cities as well as structures as "holy." A city or a structure is not holy in itself. It becomes holy when the presence of the holy has taken up residency in it. Even Jerusalem, described as a "holy" city, is not holy without the presence of the Holy dwelling within its gates. This area of wilderness was just as common as any other—until the presence of the Holy God was established.

The encounter with the Holy united Moses' purpose with the Lord's presence. The result was the commissioning of Moses. Not of Moses, the prince of Egypt, but of Moses, the man of God. He was commissioned to do what God had saved him for and purposed him for some eighty years earlier: he was to liberate the people of God and lead them to the possession of their promise from God.

As God began to unfold His plan, He told Moses that He wanted him to go back to Egypt and confront the Pharaoh with a message of deliverance concerning His people, Israel. No doubt Moses began to have flashbacks of the past, but that was in his mind, crystal clear. Memories of events that took place that caused him to run for his life. God told Moses that he had been chosen to deliver the message and deliver His people.

It didn't take Moses long to realize that he had no desire to go back to Egypt. He tried, albeit to no avail, to excuse himself from his commission repeatedly. After pulling out the last of his excuses and realizing that there was no other option, Moses asked the Lord who he should tell the people of Israel it was that had sent him with this deliverance message. After all, Moses probably still didn't have a very good reputation among the Hebrew populous. The Lord replied, "I AM that I AM." He told Moses to tell the Israelites that I AM sent you. God would not send Moses out in his own name or in his own ability and strength. That would have been certain failure.

The Hebrew term for "I AM THAT I AM" is "EHEYEH ASHER EHEYEH." It means that God is who or what He is! It means that God is eternal. He exists all by Himself without assistance. He is the ever-present and everlasting God. He is God alone. The Apostle Paul said in Acts 17:28 that in Him alone, we live, move, and have our being. But He who is the I AM, lives, moves, and exists all by Himself.

With Moses' bag of excuses now empty, and apprehension set aside, Moses began the journey back to Egypt.

THE DELIVERER

If you stop and think about it, Moses had the same anointing on him that Jeremiah had. In Jeremiah Ch.1, God commissioned the Prophet, telling him not to be afraid of the faces of the people that he was sent to speak to. The Lord assured Jeremiah that He was going to be with him every step of the way to help him and to keep him from the evil intentions of his enemies. God had told Moses the same thing. He told him not to be afraid to go back to Egypt. The Lord assured Moses that He would be with him and that He would help and keep him.

I love what the Lord says to Jeremiah in Ch.1:9-10. Jeremiah said that the Lord put forth His hand and touched his mouth (Oh that the Lord would put forth His hand and touch our mouth!). Then the Lord said to the Prophet that He had placed His Word in the Prophet's mouth; and that He had set him over nations and kingdoms of this world to root out, pull down, destroy, throw down—and then to plant and build. Notice that the first four things Jeremiah was anointed to do here were violent actions: but before the Kingdom could be built and planted, anything that stands against God and His Word must be removed.

God said to Moses in Ex.4:12 "Now therefore go, and I will be with your mouth, and I will teach you what to say." Surely God set Moses over nations and kingdoms. He set him over the Egyptians, the Canaanites, The Hittites, the Amorites, and so many more! When Israel would arrive in the promised land, they were to do what God told Jeremiah to do: root out, pull down, destroy, and throw down the heathen nations along with their idolatry and wickedness; then, Israel was to build the nation, and plant the Kingdom God within its borders. Just like light cannot cohabitate with darkness (one is sacrificed of the other), the Kingdom of God cannot cohabitate with the kingdoms of this world (again, the one is sacrificed of the other).

Now that Moses' purpose had been made one with the Lord's presence and having received the commission, Moses was ready for the next phase of his calling—confronting the Pharaoh with the demand of God to let His people go! And then bringing the people of God out of captivity and leading them to their promise.

God's message to the Pharaoh would not take a team of legal scholars to interpret. It didn't require the retention of a law firm that specializes in contractual interpretation. In fact, the Lord's message to the Pharaoh was not complicated at all. It contained one simple demand "Let my people go!" God viewed the Israelites as His people and the Pharaoh as an adversary that wrongfully held His people captive; therefore, He demanded their unconditional release.

In Ex.6, God promised Moses that the Pharaoh would let His people go. In Ex.6:1, the Lord said, "Now you will see what I will do unto the Pharaoh: for with a strong hand the Pharaoh will let them go, and with a strong hand the Pharaoh will drive them out of his land." What God was telling Moses was that the Pharaoh would not let Israel go without a fight but he would most certainly let them go.

When God's presence became united with Moses' purpose, the result was Moses became a force to be reckoned with. He went from a would-be deliverer to the man of God who would deliver a nation. God manifested Himself, His power, through signs, wonders, and miracles that not only positioned Israel for liberation; but enabled them to spoil their captors as well as recover everything that had been stolen from them.

Presence with purpose caused the Red Sea to part, allowing Israel to cross on dry ground, and drown the Pharaoh and his army. Presence with purpose led Israel by a cloud and by fire. Presence with purpose caused water to flow from a rock. Presence with purpose provided food in the wilderness. Presence with purpose provided, defended, instructed, healed, judged, and justified. It placed God's grace and favor on them and so much more!

Ex.33:11 says that presence with purpose caused the Lord to speak with Moses face to face, as a man would talk with his friend. But Moses wasn't done yet. He refused to be satisfied with just the presence. He knew there was more, and he wanted it. He wanted to go deeper. He understood the pulse of the Psalmist when he wrote in Ps.42:7, saying that deep calls out unto deep. The Lord heard Moses cry go a little deeper, a little further.

God called Moses through the ankle-deep, knee-deep, waist-deep, and a depth of God's glory that was limitless and inexhaustible. Even so, Lord!

When Moses' purpose was intertwined with the Lord's presence, it provoked Moses to desire to go beyond the presence and to step into the realm of His glory that had previously been unknown. The result was that when he came down from a mountain encounter with God, he was so illuminated by the glory that he had to cover his face with a veil to keep from blinding those who looked at him.

Finally, when Moses' purpose became one with the Lord's presence, God revealed His nature, character, and reputation (who He is and what He does) in ways that had not been known since the time on the garden. Presence with purpose defined Moses not only as a man of God...but also as a friend of God. Truly Moses could sing, "I am a friend of God; He called me 'friend'." The Lord's servants are many...but His friends are few...

Chapter Five

The Strongman's Weakness

THE BOOK OF JOSHUA RECORDS Israel's entrance, conquest, and occupation of the land God had sworn to Abraham to give to his descendants as an inheritance forever. After the death of Joshua, God raised up Judges in Israel whose responsibility was to govern, guide, defend, and avenge the people of this newly formed nation. The times and events of this period in Israel's history remind me of a somewhat less than enjoyable roller coaster ride with its ups, downs, and the seemingly out-of-control twists and turns. But unlike roller coasters that take you on a short spin around the confines of their track until you've reached the place where the ride began. For Israel, it seemed that the ride they were on would never end. Just when they thought their time on this "Twilight Zone-esque" thrill ride was finally cruising to a stop before they could exit the cars they were seated in, it would suddenly, and without warning, take them out for another ride.

In almost every theme park, roller coasters are one of the main attractions. Have you ever noticed that they all have very cool-sounding and intimidating names? It seems the more ominous the name, the greater the attraction to it. Every coaster has a name, something that it is called by. They also have a reputation, something they are known for—either by reality or allusion. This "coaster" that Israel was on and couldn't seem to find their way off of had a name and a reputation as well. This coaster was appropriately named "Rebellion." Its reputation was one of making its riders spiritually blind, deaf, and disoriented. During the period of the

Judges, Israel experienced this coaster ride frequently, whether they wanted to or not.

Judges 13:1 tells us that once again, the children of Israel had done evil in the sight of the Lord. In other words, the Lord was watching and saw what they were doing—and what they were doing displeased Him greatly. They had become rebellious and disobedient. The word "again" connects the events of the present time with that of a former. Because of their disobedience, they would once again hear that unwelcome but all too familiar voice that would say, "Please stay seated with your arms and legs in the car and your seatbelt securely fastened while the ride is in motion and until it has come to a complete stop." And with a jerk, the coaster would climb up the long, steep hill, and they would once again hold on for dear life!

Since arriving in God's promised land, Israel had exchanged the position of being the conqueror to being the conquered on several occasions due to their repeated rebellions, repentances, and reconciliations with God and His covenant. This, too, would be the result of Israel having the purpose of God but not having His presence.

CAUTION: USE ONLY AS DIRECTED BY MANUFACTURER

Judges 13 also begins the story of Samson. Samson's purpose was made known to his mother by angelic annunciation before his birth. The angel told her that she would conceive and bear a son: but there was a familiar obstacle that lay between her and the fulfillment of the angel's word. Familiar, because just like Sarah, and her daughter-in-law, Rebekah, her womb was closed, and she was unable to conceive. This time, however, the angel addressed this issue of barrenness from the beginning, telling her that God would open her womb, allowing her to conceive and give birth to a son.

As I said before, I was in the delivery room when all four of my sons were born. As they presented themselves for the first time to the world, I noticed that there were two things that were very apparent. First, they were naked. Second, they did not come with an instruction manual. How often in their growing up years did I search for an "on and off" switch, but without success. I had hoped that as I examined them, I would find a hidden compartment containing a "how to" or a "trouble shooting" manual, something—but to no avail. It seems to me that I could have avoided a lot of dumb mistakes if they had come with that little gem known as the "Instruction Manual."

Not so with Samson. The angel gave Samson's mother an instruction manual for him. He was to have a Nazarite vow on him from the womb. Having a Nazarite vow meant that Samson was to be devoted and consecrated to God for His purpose. The angel disclosed the contractual agreements contained in a Nazarite vow. He was not to drink fermented wine, eat anything unclean, and last, but certainly not least, he was not to cut his hair…ever.

He also told Samson's mother about his purpose. Because of Israel's rebellion, God had caused them to be in the hand, or under the oppressive rule, of the Philistines for forty years. For four decades, the Philistines vexed, frustrated, and tormented Israel. Samson's purpose was to deliver Israel out of their hand and liberate the people of God.

Samson was born with purpose, presence, and a full head of hair!

Long, dark, thick, and wavy hair. No extensions or visits to a hair club for men was necessary. It was all-natural; it was all his. The Bible says that as Samson grew, the Lord blessed him, and his Spirit moved on him. The word move comes from the Hebrew "pa'am," which means to tap or agitate. Samson's purpose was connected to the Lord's presence, and the Lord would tap him in his spirit. He would agitate him: He was equipping and directing him toward his purpose.

LOVE CHOOSES YOU!

Now, it happened in Samson as it does in many a young man; that Samson reached the age where he wanted to find a girl, marry, settle down, and maybe even start a family. Samson's purpose connected to God's presence caused him to be moved by the Spirit, and just as the Lord would have planned, a young, beautiful girl captured the attention of Samson and his heart.

However, as far as his parents were concerned, all they could see was a fly in the ointment. I have come to realize that more often than not, you don't choose love; love chooses you! That's why when we look at love, love sometimes doesn't seem to make any sense at all. A great example of this would be God's love for us. Our love didn't choose Him; His love chose us! Love chose Samson too.

Still, Samson's mother and father must have thought it a bit strange that he would bypass all of the eligible young ladies in Israel and fancy a girl who was of Philistine descent. Like many parents have done over the years, Samson's parents tried to talk him out of his choice for a mate…but unlike many children who may have made the mistake of marrying the wrong person, Samson's marriage was an 'arranged' marriage. It had been arranged by God Himself. God intended this marriage to be the first step toward the deliverance of His chosen people: and it became a part of Samson's purpose. Finally, like many parents, even though they didn't understand it, they went along with it, hoping for the best, but expecting the worst.

I remember when Val and I were dating. It was a wonderful time. She was a junior in high school when we met. I remember how I couldn't wait for her to get out of school so I could visit with her.

Her beautiful brown eyes, long brown hair, and perfectly tanned skin captivated my attention and dominated my conversation.

At that point, it seemed that life was all about her (well, her and the Lord) and I wanted to spend as much time with her as I could. This is how young Samson felt about this Philistine girl.

EVEN LIONS CAN HAVE A BAD DAY

Once, Val and I were having a conversation about what kind of animal we would like to be if we had been created an animal. She chose a cat although neither of us was a "cat" person. Her reasoning? She would want to be waited on and pampered. She could lay on a window sill in the sun all day and sleep. She could stroll around the house with attitude and bratty behavior, and it would be totally acceptable, after all, she's a cat! I, on the other hand, if I had been created an animal, would like to have been a lion. Why? Well, I would like to say that there is a spiritual connection. You know, like with Jesus being the Lion of Judah and all: but truthfully, there is a much less spiritual answer…my apologies.

Yep. Normally I'd say that if you had to have been created an animal, a lion would have been about as good as it could get. I mean, after all, there's that whole top-of-the-food chain thing! As animals go, any day as a lion would have been a better day than any day being, O, say, a sloth or a warthog. Can I get an "Amen!"? Any day as a lion would have been pretty much a good day…except for this particular day.

While on his way to pay his future bride a visit, the Bible says that Samson encountered a young, hungry lion. As Samson and the lion squared off, the Bible says that the Spirit, the presence of God, came upon Samson, and he tore the lion in two with his bare hands! After rending the lion, Samson dusted himself off and continued on his way to see his girl. As he was returning home, he passed by the lion, and he saw that bees had gathered on the carcass, using it as a hive. He noticed that there was an abundance of honey ready for the taking, and take, he did.

THE WEDDING

Val and I have been married now for several decades, and after all this time, the events of our big day are still very fresh. I remember waking up early that Saturday morning in May and being so nervous.

I was so nervous that I went for a ten-mile run, trying to burn off some of the nervous energy and calm myself down. I remember meeting the groomsmen at the church and, while we were dressing in our tuxedos, the jokes they were making at my expense, and their laughter seemed to me like pouring gasoline on an already raging fire of internal fear and mental unrest. I thought about how well these guys, who I thought were my friends would have fit right in with Job's friends. In fact, I drew the conclusion that my friends must have descended from his friends. Plainly put, I have never been so afraid of anything in my life. Not Val, though. She was cool, calm, and collected. She was ready.

This was Samson. He was cool, calm, collected, and ready. The courtship process was now over. All of the preliminary customs had been satisfied. The big day had arrived: the day that Samson and the "love of his life" were about to tie the knot. On the wedding day, a feast had been prepared. It was during the reception that Samson proposed a riddle to their thirty guests, all from the bride's side, that had come to the ceremony. The payment for answering the riddle was thirty fine linen shirts and thirty changes of outer clothing. If they could not answer Samson's riddle, then they would pay the same to him. The time limit for answering the riddle was seven days.

The Philistine guests found themselves three days into the feast and still no closer to finding the answer to Samson's riddle than they were when it had been first spoken. So, crafty as they were, they came up with a plan. They went to Samson's wife and told her that if she didn't get the answer to the riddle and give it to them within the remaining four days, they were going to burn her and her father's house. Sounds reasonable. They accused her of inviting them to the wedding so that she and Samson could get a few more wedding gifts from them.

The Bible says in Judges 14:16 that this threat against Samson's wife and family caused her to weep in painful sorrow. Without telling Samson about the threat made to her family, she pressed him like only a wife can to give her the answer to the riddle. He refused. It seems that from the very beginning, there were already issues with trust. She accused Samson of hating her, telling him that if he really loved her, he would tell her the answer to the riddle. Finally, the strong man could take no more of her constant pressing. He told her the answer, and she, in turn, told the Philistines.

On the final day, before the sun set, they came to Samson with the answer to his riddle. Now, there was only the matter of payment to be made to these Philistine "farmers."

How do I know that they were all farmers? Samson accused them all of "plowing with his heifer." This was a term describing their use of his wife to their advantage in order to get the answer. This term also tells us that the girl Samson was married to was extremely manipulative, untrustworthy, stubborn, selfish, untamed, and unfaithful. When the Philistine farmers told Samson the answer to the riddle, he knew immediately that it was his wife that had told them.

Since there were no local men's stores in the town where the wedding took place and his purpose was to deliver Israel from Philistine oppression; Samson was going to have to get creative in order to pay off his gambling debt. Judges 14:19 says that the Spirit, the presence of the Lord, connected with Samson's purpose, and he went down to the Philistine city of Ashkelon and went "shopping." Samson slew thirty men and took their shirts and tunics and brought them back to these agriculturalists, and paid his debt.

Ashkelon was twenty-three miles from Timnah, where the wedding took place. He went to Ashkelon because it was an influential city where the powerful and wealthy folk lived. Also, he knew that it was far enough away that he would not have been suspected of the killing of thirty Philistine men. After paying his debt, Samson would never again see his wife. Before the consummation of the wedding on the seventh night, Samson went back to Zorah, where his parents lived, and unbeknownst, his wife became a consolation prize for Samson's best man.

Samson's Change of Heart

After a period of separation, Samson had it in his heart to try and patch things up with his wife—to reconcile, not knowing that she had been given to his former best man. Where we men would bring flowers accompanied with an apology, Samson brought her a goat along with an apology. Upon his arrival in Timnah, he discovered that she was now another man's wife, and again, God would use this as an occasion to manifest Samson's purpose as a deliverer of His people.

It was the time of harvest in Philistia. Normally, it's a time of joy and excitement; a time of harvest. It meant food in their homes and on their tables. Like any civilization, wheat was crucial to their survival. The wheat had grown tall, golden brown, and full of kernels. But their excitement was to be short-lived. Samson was back in town. He was looking for revenge, but God was looking for liberation.

Judges 15:4 says that Samson caught three hundred foxes and tied their tails together by pair. He placed firebrands, burning pieces of wood between the fox's tails, and sent them running through the wheat fields, setting it on fire, and destroying their entire wheat crop. But he wasn't finished yet. Along with the wheat, he sent the foxes into the cornfields, the olive groves, and the grape vineyards. The fire spread quickly through the fields, and in a moment, it was all gone! It was Samson's revenge… one farmer to another.

The Philistine rulers were outraged. They demanded to know who had done such a thing. When they discovered that it was Samson and that it was his way of avenging himself of his wife, the Philistine rulers ordered the death of her and her father. Their reason for doing this was to punish Samson. They attacked what Samson loved. He might have been angry with his wife for her betrayal, but he still loved her. They must have thought at this point that it was over. But what they didn't realize was that Samson was just getting started.

A BIG THING IN A SMALL PACKAGE

I don't believe that Samson was a particularly large man. I don't think that he spent hours in the gym working out and pumping up his muscles: nor do I believe that he spent time down at the corner dojo learning some kind of martial art.

I think just the opposite to be true. I believe that he had an ordinary type of frame, and that's what made his appearance so unassumingly deceptive. Samson understood that his strength did not come from him at all; it came from the presence of God that was on his life.

Samson continued his revenge, but this time it was directed towards the very ones who had killed his wife and her father. Samson was ready for reconciliation with his wife, and these men had prevented that from happening.

Samson literally took the matter of revenge into his own hands.

The Bible doesn't say just how many Philistines Samson slew at this time, but it does say that it was a brutal attack that yielded a great slaughter which suggests that there were many Philistines involved in all of this. After the dust settled, Samson was the only one left standing. He then went on a two-mile hike where there was a jagged and tall, fortress-like outcropping of rock formations known as Etam. He climbed up on a rock and rested.

When the Philistines heard what had happened and how Samson had killed so many of them, they came out against Israel, ready for a fight. A delegation of Israeli men asked these Philistines why they had come in such a manner to which they replied that they had come for Samson. He had become Philistia's most wanted man, and they would not rest until they had taken him into custody.

THE POSSE

The men of Israel formed a posse of three thousand men and rode to the rock Etam that day with one goal: to bring back Samson and hand him over to the Philistines. When they found him, they asked him something to the effect of "What in the world are you thinking!? Are you out of your mind? Are you trying to get us all killed? Don't you realize that the Philistines rule over us?" Samson knew that they should never have been in the position of being ruled by the Philistines in the first place, and he also knew that it was their frequent rebellions against God that caused them to be ruled by such base and evil men. The Philistines were outwardly what Israel had become inwardly toward God. Samson almost casually replies, "I have only done to them what they have done to me."

The leaders of the posse told Samson that they were going to have to bring him in. They were going to tie him up and hand him over to the Philistines. Samson was a more than willing participant in this because his purpose felt the connection with God's presence, and he knew that He was going to use this as an occasion to bring His chosen people one step closer to their freedom. Samson made them swear to him that no one in the posse would try to hurt him—he didn't want to hurt them. An agreement was reached, and the posse along with their prisoner by choice returned to Lehi, where the Philistines were ready to take possession of their prisoner back to Philistia. The almost crazy thing about all of this was that Samson could not have been happier.

When the Israelite posse arrived with Samson, the Bible says the Philistines began to call him names: they cursed him and cursed him by their gods. Cursing Samson was an idea—not a very good one—but it was an idea! It would prove to be a decision that they would soon come to regret. It kind of reminds me of the Incredible Hulk—you wouldn't like him when he's angry! The Philistines were not going to like Samson much either because he was about to get angry.

Just when they thought they had him; the purpose-presence connection kicked in high gear. Samson broke the ropes like they were nothing. He found a donkey's jawbone, clocked in, and went to work. It would be a productive day at the office for Samson. Before anyone could know exactly what or how it happened, a thousand Philistines were already lying on the ground, dead. I wonder how far they had gotten into the fight before they realized they were outnumbered one to a thousand!

WHAT DID YOU SAY YOUR NAME WAS?

When I was in high school, they had just implemented a new physical education program in our school—boxing. I decided that it might be a good idea for me to take this class (which, as it turns out, was sort of a mistake). I was always kind of a husky fellow (big boned, they used to call it). And because of this, it often fell my lot to spar with our boxing coach, who just happened to be a former middleweight champion. I won't try to describe to you what it was like when he hit me because, honestly, I don't remember much. My memories are mostly confined to that of being brought back to consciousness with the aid of smelling salts stuck in my nose: and even after the salts had worked their magic, it still seemed like a thick fog had rolled in from off the coast, and I just happened to have been caught in it. I would hear them call my name, but it took some time for the fog to lift and for me to understand that it was my name that they were calling.

It didn't take but one semester for me to come to the conclusion that maybe boxing just wasn't for me. However, I have one other memory of my boxing days. We went 3 three-minute rounds. By the time the second round was winding down, my arms felt like led. My brain would scream electrical impulse signals to them to come up and block the onslaught of punches being thrown my way, but both arms remained in total rebellion! I could not get them up for anything, nor could I get them to do anything.

Thus, my encounters with the mat, which smelled very sweaty, were more frequent than I'd like to remember: and then there was the occasional question raised by other classmates, "Is he dead?"

When Samson had finished this fight with the Philistines, he was thirsty, very thirsty. I mean, really, who wouldn't be thirsty after a fight like the one Samson had just had. The presence of God responded by turning the jawbone he fought with into a fountain. God opened a hole in the bone, and cool, refreshing water came out of it quenching Samson's thirst. Throughout the Bible, we find examples of where God was very good at quenching the thirst of those who are thirsty.

EVERY SUPERMAN HAS THEIR KRYPTONITE

We all know the story of Superman, right? We know how his planet Krypton was about to be destroyed, and his parents placed him in a spacecraft and sent him to Earth, where he became a superhero defending the people of Earth. Superman had one weakness, kryptonite. Kryptonite was supposed to be a rock that somehow made it from Krypton to Earth after it had exploded. Every time Superman would come in contact with kryptonite, it would sap his strength, leaving him weak, helpless, and vulnerable. Superman had his kryptonite, and so did Samson. Superman's kryptonite came from his planet, and so did Samson's. Superman's kryptonite was a rock; Samson's kryptonite was women.

He is not alone in this, though. Many a man has been bound, weakened, manipulated, and even destroyed by this earthly kryptonite that God Himself called woman. Solomon speaks as an authority on this subject when he warns and advises men on how to handle this type of kryptonite in the Book of Proverbs.

Several years ago, I was speaking with a pastor friend of mine, and we were discussing marriage issues. I had made a comment about what Solomon said in Proverbs 18:22 when he wrote, "He that finds a wife finds a good thing and obtains favor from the Lord." I said to my friend, "Notice, Solomon said he that finds a wife, finds a good thing: not just a woman, but a wife." I continued, "Every female is a woman, but not every woman is a wife."

I told him that men of God need to look for a wife, not just a woman: and that they need to know the difference between the two.

Likewise, women need to know the difference between a man and a husband. Understanding the difference and being jealous of yourself and of your future can be the difference between magic and misery.

WEAKNESS FOUND AN ENTRANCE

Samson went down to Gaza, a Philistine city, and the first thing he did was to place himself in a room with his kryptonite, a woman; who also happened to be a harlot. This would be Samson's second encounter with his personal kryptonite. His first was his Philistine wife, and now, a Philistine harlot. As he entered the city, somebody recognized him from the wanted posters that were plastered on the walls of the buildings in every city throughout Philistia. The one who recognized him was quick to report their sighting to the city officials. They surrounded the house Samson entered and spent the night awaiting his departure.

Their plan was to take him as he left the harlot's house and kill him. He stayed at the house until midnight. Somehow Samson became aware of their plan. The Bible says that at midnight, the Spirit of the Lord came on him, and he escaped. But on his way out, he ripped up the gates that kept the city's entrance, along with the posts they were fastened to, and carried them to the top of a hill, where he dropped them. These gates were large wood doors weighing hundreds of pounds each. They were closed at night to protect the city against enemy attacks carried out under the cover of darkness.

THERE'S JUST SOMETHING ABOUT THOSE PHILISTINE WOMEN!

There are a few things that I think are very clear from the story of Samson in the Book of Judges. Not the least of which is the fact that Samson had a thing for the femme fatale of Philistia. Again, it doesn't take an optometrist to see that he was drawn to these types of women like a moth to a streetlight on a hot and muggy summer's night. There was an attraction, and eventually, it would prove to be a fatal one. His countrymen couldn't understand it. His own parents couldn't figure it out, but as we read through his story, we see that somehow this thing that Samson had for Philistine women was used by God to complete Samson's purpose.

The Bible does not say anything about how Samson met Delilah. It begins this part of the story simply by saying that Samson loved Delilah. Samson thought his ex-wife was pretty, and there was no doubt that in some sense of the word, he loved her. But his attraction to her was, for the most part, physical. He went into the harlot out of convenience, but he loved Delilah. Delilah was a material girl who really couldn't have cared less about Samson. She loved things, and she was not above using whatever means was at her disposal to get what she wanted. She was cunning, manipulative, deceptive, arrogant, impudent, uncaring, selfish, and greedy. She moved through her world undetected, like a crocodile moves through the clouded waters of a murky river.

A crocodile will move almost effortlessly just beneath the surface of the water, searching for its next meal. Many times, crocodiles cannot be detected by their prey until they are ready to strike. When they find their victim, they will lunge out of the water and catch their quarry by surprise: its target becomes dazed and confused. With their mouths, they latch onto their prey with bone-crushing force. Then, going into a "death roll," they tear their helpless victim apart, and will not stop until they have consumed it in its entirety.

THE CROC WHO WORE LIPSTICK

Delilah had a "crocodile spirit." She, too, would navigate just beneath the surface of the murky waters of purpose without presence. She would fix her eyes on her next victim, and before they knew what hit them, she would strike at them and take from them everything she could get: and having devoured them, she would take a small portion of what was left of her victim, and display it as her latest trophy. Samson loved Delilah, and Delilah loved that Samson loved her—it made her job much easier. She could and would use it to her advantage, and use it she did.

Samson didn't realize it, but he was about to be taken for a ride on the back of a deceptive Croc named Delilah. It would be a ride that would take him from the sure footing of the riverbank into the instability of the deep waters where a croc, like Delilah, can move with precision and deadly accuracy. She would take him on a journey that, for the first time, would lead him out of the place of purpose with presence, and into the muddy waters of presence-less purpose. This journey would end up being a costly one for Samson.

When he was most vulnerable, she would strike, fast and decisively; and although Samson would come to know that Delilah was the croc that bit him, but until he had been bitten, he would never see it coming.

Why? Because he allowed himself to be carried out of the presence on the back of a deceptive and ruthless predator who would devour him, and leave him broken and with nothing more than hollow purpose.

The lords of the Philistines knew all too well the character and reputation of Delilah. They were no stranger to who she was, what she was, and what she was capable of. Maybe even some of them had at one time or another been bitten by the craftiness that she had devised and perfected through greed and selfish ambition. Maybe they too had paid for their foolish encounters with her. If so, she would see to it that they would pay again, and they would pay dearly. Maybe, under any other circumstances, they would be inclined to keep their distance from her, but they were desperate. They were not above conspiring with Delilah to once and for all trap Samson who remained public enemy number one on Philistia's most wanted list.

When the lords of the Philistines knew that Samson loved Delilah, and knowing Delilah the way they did, they were almost beside themselves with excitement. At last, they could lift up their heads, look into the distance, and see what appeared to be a faint glimmer of light signaling that they could be near the end of this long, dark tunnel.

The money and the challenge of overcoming the strongman was more than Delilah could resist. Her job was a simple one really. Find out the source of Samson's strength and neutralize it. Once their target had been neutralized, they would take it from there. The payment: fifty-five hundred pieces of silver. With the guarantee of payment in place, Delilah set out to find the source of Samson's strength, steal it from him, and deliver him into the hands of the Philistine rulers.

According to Judges 16:6, Delilah didn't waste any time. She planned her work carefully, and then she worked her plan. She determined that the best way to compromise her target would be through "deceptive honesty." When we read the story from our vantage point, we think, "How could you not see this, Samson?" To us, what she was doing is very plain to see; but remember, Samson wasn't privileged to have our vantage point; He was in love.

The Apostle Paul wrote in 1Cor.13:7 that love bears all things, believes all things, hopes all things, and endures all things. Samson's love for Delilah caused him to bear, believe, and endure all things. It clouded his discernment as well as his judgment. Love caused him to become imbalanced and irrational. Delilah would sense this weakness in Samson and callously exploit it to her advantage. She could see him clearly; she could read him like a book. However, Samson could only see what Delilah was willing to show him which was nothing more than an illusion. She had him in her sights and began to slowly lure him closer to the water's edge and then into the murky waters of purpose without presence.

LET'S GET THIS OVER WITH ALREADY!

Delilah didn't want to waste any time. After all, fifty-five hundred pieces of silver waiting on her along with the prestige that would accompany her as the one who finally brought Philistia's nemesis, Israel's strongman to his knees. Added to this was the matter of her legacy that would live on throughout future Philistine generations. Songs would be sung about her. Books would be written glorifying her shrewdness and bravery. With her plan in place, she immediately began to move in for the kill.

Operation codename "Deceptive Honesty" was a go. She would say in an innocent and sincere tone, "Tell me, Samson, what is the source of your great strength, and how can you be subdued?" Samson, not wanting to divulge his secret too quickly, told her a lie.

What Samson didn't realize in all of this, was that as he drew closer to Delilah, the farther away the presence moved from him. Actually, the presence began to move away from him when he decided to spend the evening with the harlot. He felt "okay" with it because, you know, it wasn't like he ate some pork ribs, or drank wine, or touched dead things, or…got a haircut. But now he found himself lying about the source of his strength, and the presence moved a little further away.

Some of us would think that after he told her that if his arms were bound together with seven green cords, that he would be as weak as any man: and she tied his arms with said cords, then maybe, just maybe, we'd be suspicious, right? Not our hero! Why? Because as the presence moved away from Samson, so did his ability to discern good and evil as well.

When Delilah was "fishing" in Samson's pond, the Philistines took up positions around the house anxiously awaiting the moment when they could burst in through the door, and take Israel's strongman captive.

They had rehearsed it over and over: they dreamt of this moment—and now, they were so close to it they could almost taste their victory…almost.

After she tied him up, she cried, "The Philistines are upon you!" as though she was warning him; but in reality, she was fishing, to see if this was indeed the secret to Samson's strength. Well, as it turns out, it was not. Samson lied, and the presence moved a little further away.

Even though she was unsuccessful in her first attempt, she remained undaunted in her objective—she was determined to discover the source of Samson's strength. "You've planned your work, now work your plan," she would tell herself. In Judges 16:10, there is some great irony if you're into that sort of thing. Delilah accused Samson of mocking her! Her entire relationship with Samson was a mockery. Now, he is playing the same game that she was, and she accuses him of mockery.

She demands that Samson tell her the source of his great strength, but this time, she wants the truth; which is also irony because there was no truth in her. Samson answers her with another lie, with the same result. Delilah still doesn't know the source of Samson's strength. The Philistines that were sent to secure him are still empty handed and waiting...and the presence, along with discernment, has again moved a little farther away.

A third time this scenario would play itself out, the demand to know, the lie to cover, the accusation of trickery made by Delilah, and the expectant Philistine garrison who were waiting. The presence that had been connected with Samson's purpose from conception was now moving farther and farther away from him.

In verse fifteen of Ch.16, Delilah takes out an emotional dagger and thrusts it straight into the heart of Samson. She said in effect, "You tell me that you love me, but every time you tell me this, you lie to me! I have asked you three times about the source of your strength and how you can become like any other man; and all you've done was mock me and disrespect me."

Even though Delilah's words were the product of a well-designed and flawlessly executed conspiracy against Samson, it still cut deep into his heart. Day after day she pressed him; she vexed his soul by her constant demand to know the source of his strength. Over and over, day after day, she would make her demand of him. Through her relentless pursuit of the source, Samson had come to the point where he just wanted to die. As I read through this, the thought came to me, "why didn't Samson just leave her? They weren't married. He could have just walked away, couldn't he?" When the presence left Samson, his discernment left with it, along with his ability to reason. He was caught up in an emotional, soul tie that had bound him long before Delilah ever put a razor to his head.

We must be careful who we connect our emotions—our soul with. Those ties become strong and, sometimes unbreakable, not because God is unable, but because the person caught in the bondage is not mentally or emotionally capable or willing to be jealous for themselves and fight for their victory. This is why we see people (and I've counseled dozens of them) who can't seem to break the cycle of going from one abusive relationship to another. They bound their soul to an abusive spirit that controls them and their relationship's.

Samson's kryptonite had weakened him long before the locks of his hair were shaved off. This is why it is so important that we cut ties with anything that desires to steal our purpose and separate the Lord's presence from us. The presence is the anointing of the Holy Spirit. Samson "gave in" long before he came clean concerning the source of his strength. It is imperative that we remain jealous for ourselves and for our future with a godly jealousy.

Samson finally told Delilah about his Nazarite vow: How a razor had never touched his head, and that if he was to lose his hair, he would lose his strength as well and become as weak as any man. This time, Delilah knew that she had him. She lay Samson's head on her lap and, pretending to comfort him, she cradled him to sleep. Samson was emotionally, and now physically, exhausted. He had never experienced physical exhaustion before: he didn't recognize the feeling therefore he couldn't define it. The time had come, and Delilah wasted no time. With Samson fast asleep, she finally had her chance, and moved in for the kill.

She gently laid Samson's head on a pillow so that she would not wake him, and then she quietly walked into her sewing room. She knew just where to find the tool that she needed to dismantle the strength of Samson: one lock of hair at a time. She took hold of a razor and walked back into the room where Samson slept. Samson was not only physically asleep, but because the presence moved away from him, he was spiritually asleep as well. While his body and spirit slept, Delilah disabled Samson both physically and spiritually with one fell swoop of the razor. With his hair now cut, the covenant was broken and the presence was gone. As the presence of the Lord departed completely, so did Samson's strength. He had purpose without presence, and he truly became like any other man.

This time, when Delilah woke Samson, and as she had done three times before, she claimed that the Philistines were there to take him. The Bible says that Samson awoke, as he had done before, and said, "I will go out as at other times before and shake myself." The word "shake" means to tell or to roar like a lion and to run like a wild man toward the enemy. This time it would be different though. He was unaware that as he slept, the presence had departed, and he was left alone with only his purpose.

Samson shook and shook until he was all shook up...and, nothing. Suddenly he found himself surrounded by the Philistines. For the first time in his life, instead of overcoming, he was overcome. Confusion; questions ran through his mind—but were unaccompanied by answers. It was like his mind; his thoughts had been placed in a blender and Delilah had flipped on the switch.

The first thing the Philistines did to Samson was to gouge out his eyes, blinding him. They brought him to Gaza, where they bound him with chains and fetters made from brass, and they made him grind wheat and corn in their prison house. The presence had been removed and all that remained was Samson's purpose. This had left him weak, blind, bound, broken, and enslaved. His physical condition testified of his spiritual condition. It was a reflection of it. Physical weakness was the allusion— spiritual weakness was the reality. The Philistines were in control now. They had abused, mocked, and humiliated Samson. His condition left him unable to complete the purpose that God had given him from the moment the angel came and visited his mother all those years ago—until, his hair began to grow back.

Who knows exactly whose fault it was: or where to place the blame? Surely the lords of the Philistines would not forget to place someone in charge of making sure that Samson's hair would forever remain short. If it had been me, I would have placed a barber with the sole responsibility of making sure Samson's hair did not grow back. If it had been my job to cut Samson's hair, there would have been weekly haircuts. Somebody had dropped the shears as it were, and the only consolation would come from the fact that none of them would live long enough to regret it.

As God would have it, Samson's hair did indeed begin to grow back again and with its growth, came a renewal of Samson, the man of God and deliverer of Israel. Along with his renewed hair, came a renewed mind, a renewed spirit, and a renewed Nazarite covenant with God. I am sure that while Samson turned that great stone wheel, one revolution at a time, he had spent a lot of time thinking about how different things would have been had he not allowed himself to be overcome by his personal kryptonite or had he not taken that ride on the back of that croc named Delilah. No doubt he thought about how it all cost him the presence.

He wished that he had made better choices. He lived with regret on a daily basis. I believe this to be true because of the words he spoke in his final request to God. What a blessing it is to know that through faith in Jesus and obedience to His Word, we have been positioned to live a regret-free life. Samson certainly spent quite a while serving the unprofitable choices that he made. I'm also sure that it was during this time that repentance, reconciliation, and restoration had taken place. As his hair grew, so did the presence. Every day his hair got a little longer; the presence came a little closer.

THE PARTY ALWAYS ENDS

Everybody likes a party, and the Philistines were no exception. When they weren't out plundering and pillaging, they enjoyed getting together on occasion and celebrating. On this day, they thought it good to throw a party in honor of their god, Dagon, whom they ignorantly credited for delivering Samson into their hands. They never came to the understanding that it was the choices Samson made that was to be credited for his capture.

Three thousand lords, ladies, dignitaries, socialites, and various others filled the temple of Dagon on that day. It was a day of celebration.

A massive feast had been prepared by the finest of Philistia's chefs who had created culinary artistry. At this celebration they would have a special guest to provide them entertainment.

A young man would lead Samson into the arena on this day. It was just another bad decision that would be one of several that had been made by the careless Philistine rulers, and they would soon regret their carelessness. The young man chained Samson to two columns that were major structural supports for the temple of their idol god. As they ate and drank, they would gesture at Samson, laughing, mocking, and ridiculing him. They would throw food as well as other things at him and watch as he flinched while trying to dodge the onslaught of all the things being thrown in his direction. Because he was blind, he was unable to avoid much of what was thrown—he couldn't see where it was coming from.

A consecrated, dedicated, and renewed Samson would stand chained between those pillars: a Samson that once again had his purpose connected to the presence of God that had fully returned: and would move him one final time for one final act of deliverance.

Samson asked the boy to allow him to feel the pillars. He said "Just let me rest on them for a moment." With one hand on one pillar, and the other hand on the other pillar, Samson cried out to the Lord asking Him to release His presence one more time. Samson renewed his covenant with God and he was asking God to do the same. "Lord, strengthen me one more time." Samson would pray. "Avenge me. Punish them because of what they did to my eyes."

Samson began to press against the pillars, and as he pressed, they started to bow in the middle. He cried out, "Let me die with the Philistines!" And with one final push, the pillars cracked in half and the temple of Dagon imploded, killing all three thousand Philistines that were present. No matter how good the party is, at some point, the party always ends. Once ended, there would be no more.

When Samson's purpose was reconnected with God's presence, it enabled him to complete his destiny and leave a legacy. Samson's legacy reads something like this, "Thus the dead which he slew at his death were more than which he slew when he was alive."

Upon his death, Samson took his place in the Hebrews Ch.11 Hall of the Faithful. When you have come to the end of your journey, how will your legacy read? For Samson, it reads: The strongman finished strong. All for His glory!

Chapter Six

———❦———

A Famine in the House of Bread

THE BOOK OF RUTH WAS written toward the end of the period in Israel's history when God had established judges to govern His people. In this book, we read about a family who lived in the town of Bethlehem. In the Book of Ruth, we are able to see how the physical conditions in which they lived paralleled the spiritual condition of the times in which they lived.

It is the story of a man named Elimelech who lived in Bethlehem with his wife, Naomi, their two sons, Mahlon and Chilion, and their son's wives, Ruth and Orpah. Ruth talks about how having purpose without the presence caused them to make the fateful decision to leave Bethlehem, and journey eastward to the land of Moab, where they, for a season, would call home.

It describes the loss, heartache, and confusion that overcame them as a result of choosing to leave Bethlehem and relocate to the land of Moab: but thanks be to God that it doesn't end there. Ruth also describes the return, restoration, grace, and divine providence of God when purpose reconnects with presence.

The Book of Ruth is a portrait painted with the vibrant colors of Isaiah 61:3, where the Prophet writes, "To give unto them beauty for ashes, the oil of gladness for mourning, and a garment of praise for the spirit of heaviness: that they may be called the trees of righteousness, the planting of the Lord, the He might be glorified."

The grace of the Lord that has been interwoven throughout His eternal purpose for the nation of Israel would not allow His people to be forgotten nor abandoned in a strange land of presence-less purpose, but He providentially guided them back into His great presence to complete a great purpose.

NO BREAD IN THE HOUSE OF BREAD?

The name Bethlehem comes from the Hebrew word meaning House of Bread. If I were to ask you what it was that you would expect to find in abundance in a place called the House of Bread, you would probably say "bread." Certainly, it would be our expectation to find bread in the House of Bread: but the Bible declares that there was a famine in Bethlehem, in the House of Bread.

How could it be? How did it happen? How is it that there was a famine in the House of Bread? The Bible is very clear throughout the Book of Jeremiah and in other places like Ezekiel Ch.5 and elsewhere that there is a direct correlation between disobedience and famine.

NO KING IN ISRAEL?

Judges 17:6 and Judges 21:25 say the very same thing, and they not only give us a glimpse into the physical conditions in Israel during this time but the spiritual climate as well. They both read like this "In those days, there was no king, and every man did that which was right in his own eyes." Israel had purpose as a nation, but it had a serious lack of presence. Why? Because there were no absolutes—there was no absolute "right" or "wrong." No black and white; only the grey area of individual subjectiveness.

Israel had come to a place where they had erased the line between philosophy, opinion, thought, feeling, subjective interpretation—and absolute truth. Right and wrong had become individually subjective to the one who defined it; therefore, one person's right or wrong wasn't necessarily another person's right or wrong because everyone was doing what was right or wrong as they defined it instead of how God defined it. Sound familiar? This seems to be a characteristic of our day as well. Times change, but apart from God, human nature doesn't.

By subjectively defining right and wrong, we think that we can excuse ourselves from all individual accountability and responsibility for our actions and shift the blame for them to someone or something else, thereby judging and rendering ourselves to be just innocent victims. We have mastered the art of dodging individual responsibility and accountability.

I remember several years ago listening to a local radio station, and one of the announcers was talking about road rage: and how it had been given a medical term called Intermittent Explosive Disorder or IED for short. It's no longer your fault that you, in a fit of rage, want to pull over the driver that just cut you off on the highway and give them a roadside pep talk in driving education, training, and development right there on the side of the road. No, it's not your fault! You suffer from IED.

Why do we do this? We believe that if we can assign something a name that is beyond our control; like saying alcoholism is a disease instead of a sin; or that homosexuality is a genetic predisposition instead of sin; or that lying is pathological instead of sin—we feel that we are somehow released from individual responsibility and accountability because, after all, we can't be held accountable for what we can't control. We received the "learned" behavior from Adam and Eve. If you read Gen.3, you'll see a whole lot of blame-shifting going on in the garden.

When Val and I pastored a church in Nevada, in our town, there was a reform school for young men, and I had the privilege of going there just about every Sunday afternoon to meet with these young men and invest the Word of God into them.

One afternoon, I met with a group of about fifty boys, and I asked them this question. I asked how many of them were seeing either a psychiatrist or a psychologist. Almost, if not every hand, went up into the air. Then I asked, "How many of these psychiatrists or psychologists that you are seeing have told you that the reason you are the way you are or behave the way you do is the result of something that your mama did, or your daddy did, or your uncle or aunty, or 'the man' etc. either did to you or didn't do for you? How many of you were told that you are the product of victimization?" And again, every hand that went up before went up again.

Then I said to them, "Then if you are the victim of what someone or something else did to you or didn't do for you, why aren't they here serving time instead of you? After all, you're a victim!" I continued, "Why isn't your mama here, or your daddy, or 'the man'? Why are you being punished instead of them?"

I said to these boys, "Doesn't that scream individual responsibility and accountability?" It testifies to us that there is an absolute right and an absolute wrong, and that we are personally accountable and responsible for our individual and collective actions, but only they that have ears to hear can hear the logic of truth.

We see this exemplified in the "coexist" and "tolerance" philosophies that are present in many churches throughout the United States and other countries.

The premise that everyone can do what is right in their own eyes and be right is—well, the Apostle Paul put it like this "professing themselves to be enlightened and wise, in reality, they became dull in vision and foolish in thought."

It wasn't that there was no king in Israel. God made it very clear in 1Samuel 8:7 that He was Israel's King. Surely it was not because there was no King in Israel. It was, however, that in doing right and wrong subjectively, as they defined it instead of how God defined it, they were actively refusing to acknowledge God as their King.

Purpose without presence can bring us to a place where we no longer acknowledge the Lord as our King, and what we do, even things that we do "in His name" can become right in our own eyes—but if we lack His presence, what we do is not right in His. It does not matter how we define what is right or what is wrong; it only matters how He defines them: and if our definition is different than His, we must reject ours and embrace His.

The Ephesian Church in Rev.2 is a prime example of this. Jesus said in verses 2-4 that He knew their works, their labors, and their patience. He knew how they held onto what was true and rejected what was not. He said that they had carried the burdens of those who were weak: He also said that they were busy doing things for Him and had not grown weary in the process. But then, Jesus said that He had an issue with them—they had forsaken their "first love" for Him.

Jesus acknowledged that they were busy in their Kingdom purpose. They held to the truth and shouldered the burdens of those who weren't strong enough to carry them on their own. They exercised patient endurance and exposed imposters for what they were. All of these things were recognized and commended by Jesus. But there was a problem. They had forsaken their "first love." They had walked out of the place of His presence and became left only with purpose.

Purpose without the presence will cause the Church to become nothing more than a charity organization. The Church at Ephesus had become as powerless as a secular charity to affect a Gospel change in the lives of men and women. Like many Church organizations in our day, they became just another charity handing out clothing or a sack lunch instead of releasing the life-changing force of the Kingdom of God, which is the Gospel of Jesus Christ.

We must be careful not to become so busy in conducting our purpose that we forget who we're doing it for, why we're doing it, and what we must possess in order to complete it. As we move forward towards the fulfillment of all that God has purposed for our lives and ministries, our love for God must be our highest motivation and remain our greatest priority. Otherwise, like the Church at Ephesus, the Lord will come and remove our candlestick, and the light of His presence will forever be taken away.

Disobedience, rebellion, selfish ambition, pride, breaking and redefining God's laws were all part of the spiritual and moral decline that Israel engaged in, which led them to a famine in the House of Bread.

THE SEARCH FOR BREAD

I love to look at the meaning of people's names in the Bible and see how their names often fit into their character, their purpose; and how it played a vital role in the shaping of their destiny. The story of Ruth is a wonderful example of this.

Defining the names of Elimelech, Naomi, Mahlon, and Chilion, gives us insight into the real danger of leaving the House of Bread, which is the place of His presence, and journey to the land of Moab, a place devoid of the presence but still containing purpose. To help you better understand what I am about to say, please allow me to define these four names.

The name Elimelech means: *My God is King.*
The name Naomi means: *Pleasant one.*
The name Mahlon means: *Sick.*
The name Chilion means: *Withering or pining away.*

Now, follow me. Famine in the House of Bread drove those who acknowledged God as King (Elimelech), the Pleasant ones (Naomi), into the land of Moab, which represents shame, disgrace, humiliation, and the consequence of sin. The result of leaving the House of Bread was that they became soul-sick (Mahlon), and their sickness caused them to wither and pine away (Chilion) until death bereaved the Pleasant One (Naomi) of the things she loved: her husband and her two sons.

When they walked away from the House of Bread, the Pleasant Ones walked away from their God, who was King: and because Moab represented a substitute, a fake or counterfeit House of Bread, the result was that they became physically and spiritually sick. In both body and in spirit, they withered away, and Elimelech, Mahlon, and Chilion died in a counterfeit house.

Bread should have been available in the House of Bread. But instead of Bread—there was famine. The famine in the House of Bread caused Elimelech and Naomi to take their sons and the son's wives on a journey to Moab to search for Bread. What they discovered, however, was not bread but a bread substitute. There would be no bread in Moab; only the pain and sorrow that are constant companions of sickness and death.

For several years I had the privilege of traveling to Volgograd, Russia, to teach at New Life Bible College. On my first trip, I was taken to a World War II museum that is situated along the beautiful banks of the Volga River. On the tour, our guide would take us through various stations and then begin to explain the significance of all the things that were displayed in the stations.

In one station, I recall seeing what, by appearance (size, shape, and texture), looked like a granola bar. Our tour guide began to explain what it really was. She said that during the Battle of Stalingrad (Volgograd), one million German soldiers and one million Russian soldiers died in this military campaign.

She said that as the war waged on, the Russian military was running out of food to feed the soldiers fighting against the German army. She said that what they began to do was to take sawdust and compress it, and then they would give it to the Russian troops to eat. It was not bread; it was a bread substitute. There was no nutritional value in these sawdust cakes, but the illusion was that it would take away the pain of hunger and allow the soldiers to continue to fight.

THE OVENS ARE COLD, AND THE SHELVES ARE BARE

Many of us vividly recall where we were and what we were doing when the events of Sept.11, 2001 took, place. Me? I was in La Ceiba, Honduras, preparing to minister at a pastor's conference.

After I had finished gathering all of the things that I would need for the day's conference, I went into the living room area of the mission house where the rest of the mission team and I were staying.

As I walked into the room, the television was on, and a news reporter was in real-time trying to make sense of and explain what had just happened. The North Tower had just been hit by the plane. At first, I actually thought it was a movie that some of the people who were with me were watching. I thought that they were just killing time until we were ready to head to the church for the conference. It was then that I saw the second plane as it slammed into the South Tower, and as I watched and listened to the reporter, I began to realize that this was nothing that Hollywood had produced: this was real.

I went back into my room and sat on the side of the bed, stunned by what I had just witnessed. My heart was crushed. I remember praying and telling the Lord, "How can I go and encourage these pastors when my heart has melted within me?" Honestly, it shook me to the very core of my being.

At that moment, the Lord began to release a supernatural strength in me, and we had a phenomenal day of teaching, impartation, and the edification of these precious men and women of God. Between sessions, our team members would huddle around our missionary host to hear the latest reports. For eight days after the conference had ended, we were grounded in La Ceiba because all domestic and international flights had been canceled.

I was hearing reports of churches in the U.S. that were being filled with "hungry" people who had grown tired of Moab with its bread substitutes that could not satisfy nor take away the hunger of their souls. They were hurting, fearful, and hungry, and they went looking for bread in the place where bread should have been prepared and ready to be consumed by the hungry, famished souls of those who journeyed out of Moab to the place where they thought true bread would be found, the Church.

I was told that they came by the hundreds to local Bethlehem's—Houses of Bread; only to find the ovens cold and the shelves empty. Like in the days of Ruth, there was no bread in the House of Bread: and they walked out of the "bakeries" as they walked in—hungry, thirsty, frightened, tired... and lost.

How could this be? How could there be no bread in the Church? The House of Bread! The Church has purpose, but many churches are without the presence: therefore, they have no real bread to feed the hungry soul... just a sawdust substitute that is nothing more than the illusion of bread.

This famine in the House of Bread, the Church, came through the same route that it took in Ruth's day. In those days, there was no(acknowledged) King, and every man (many in the Church) did that which was right, not in God's eyes, but their own.

With her husband and sons dead, and having been abandoned by Orpah, Naomi and her daughter in law, Ruth, would be the only ones to make it out of Moab, the land of a substitute bread; a land devoid of the presence, and return back into the land of genuine bread: the place where purpose meets presence—the place where destinies are realized, and legacies are written in stone.

Upon their return, as God would have it, Naomi discovers a relative whose name was Boaz. When purpose reconnected with presence, genuine bread replacing the artificial; God would position Ruth and Boaz to take their place in the genealogical order of Jesus Christ, who just happens to be called the Bread of Life. The Father sent this Bread from the heavenly House of Bread to satisfy the human soul's hunger. How fitting it was that the Bread of heaven, Jesus, was "baked" in Bethlehem, in the House of Bread. In the Father's House of Bread...a famine will never be.

Chapter Seven

The Trouble with Rooftop Visions

WHEN I THINK OF ONE person who possessed purpose with presence from their youth unto their death, leaving an almost flawless legacy of what could be accomplished through a determination to keep purpose and presence united and maintain the balance between the two, I think of David, Israel's greatest king.

Like Joseph of old, from a young age, the presence of the Lord was with David; and with the presence was purpose. I believe that from David's early years, he understood that the presence and purpose of God was with him, and although he didn't know how or what, he believed that one day God would use him to accomplish great things. It is no coincidence that David and the Lord were both shepherds.

LIVING WITHIN THE TWENTY-THIRD PSALM

David knew as a shepherd, that the presence of the Great Shepherd was with him to lead, protect, and provide for him as he led, protected, and provided for his sheep. He knew that presence not only delivered him from lions and bears, but it also kept him and his charge safe from a host of other predators that inhabited the wilderness as well.

The presence gave David an inner strength and bold confidence in God that set him apart from most of his contemporaries. He understood that everything he needed resided in the presence, and as long as he remained in the presence, he would have everything he needed. The presence of the Holy God continually led him from pasture to pasture and beside still waters even as he would lead his sheep to the same. He knew the presence was there to restore, refresh, reward, and rescue him. He knew the presence of God was with him when he would lie down to sleep, and it was still with him when he woke up. He knew the presence was with him when he went out; it would be with him on the journey, and it would bring him safely back home again and without loss.

David was confident that the presence would lead him on the right path toward his purpose. He believed that the Lord was a righteous God, and he was acquainted with the power of His name.

He knew that because the presence was with him, even though his journey would from time to time take him through the valley: in the darkness and obscurity of the shadows—in paths that were often dangerous, that he had no real need to fear what evil things may be lurking in the valley or hiding under the cover of the shadows. He trusted that the presence was with him before he went into the valley. He trusted it would keep him while he was in the valley: and that it would lead him out of the valley and remain with him on the other side. He was confident in His God and that His presence would never leave him or forsake him.

He believed that like his rod and staff (representing the Word and the Spirit of the Lord) was a weapon, the presence was a weapon capable of both offensive and defensive protection: as well as a tool to steady his steps—and it was a way for him to communicate with his sheep. He knew the presence to be a constant comfort and companion to him.

The young shepherd knew the presence enabled him to sit and feast at the table of God's blessings, even while the enemies of his prosperity were surrounding him. Instead of fighting and defending himself and his sheep, he rested in the reality of Isaiah 26:3, where the Prophet writes, "You will keep them in perfect peace whose mind is stayed upon You, because they trust You."

David trusted that the presence would keep him and his sheep in perfect peace because his mind was fixed on the Lord. He was continuously in David's thoughts and in his heart.

He also was confident that the presence would anoint, position, empower and facilitate the purpose of God for his life. David believed that God would welcome him into His presence because he had welcomed His presence into his. The result of which would be an abundance of the Kingdom blessings of God filling David's life and then overflowing and touching the lives of others for their blessing.

Finally, David knew that because he had God's presence, he also had his goodness and mercy and that these would always be with him no matter where his purpose would take him. He knew that the presence would be with him every day of this life and would be with him throughout eternity.

A SHEPHERD, A POET, AND A WARRIOR

Presence with purpose was the inspiration that enabled him to sit and write poetry along with hymns containing praise, petition, confession, adoration, deliverance, anticipation, and expectancy. Presence with purpose established David's kingdom in worship and fueled his pursuit of chasing after and capturing the heart of God.

David understood that at some point, God's presence would intersect with his purpose to create and shape his destiny. But in the beginning, he never would have imagined that it would take him from leading sheep to leading a nation. The presence of God that was with David connected with his purpose, and having removed Saul from being king; the presence positioned David to be anointed king over all Israel in his place.

Presence with purpose enabled David to face Goliath with a confident assurance of victory. Presence caused David to prevail over the giant and defeat him, thus delivering the enemies of Israel into their hands. Presence with purpose caused David to escape twenty-one attempts made on his life by Saul and his army. Presence kept him from the venomous words of viperous men: subtle enemies whose calculated lies were like the poison in the fangs of a deadly serpent.

The power of a poisonous serpent is in his mouth, and like serpents do when attacking prey, these serpents, these enemies of David, sought to latch themselves onto him with their mouths. They delighted in the thought of biting David with their lying words, sinking their fangs deep, and releasing their poisonous venom into his soul. Their desire was to wound him to where he could not recover, but the presence wouldn't allow it to be so.

THE PRODUCT OF PRESENCE

Presence with purpose kept David in a failed marriage to Saul's daughter, Michal. Presence with purpose gave him favor with Johnathon, Saul's son, who hid him from Saul on several occasions and, just as often, interceded on his behalf. Presence with purpose kept David when he ran from Saul and hid among the Philistines in Gath.

Presence with purpose kept David when he had been identified as David, the slayer of ten thousand Philistines by some of king Achish's servants.

Presence with purpose enabled David to give an Academy Award-winning performance as he pretended to be a madman in the court of Achish. Psalm 66 was birthed from this event in David's life.

Presence kept David in his wilderness journey. Presence kept him from the conspiracy of his son, Absalom, and one of his most trusted counselor's and friend, Ahithophel. The presence of God connected with David's purpose, training him as a warrior and enabling him to fight the armies of the Amalekites, Ammonites, Philistines, Syrians, Moabites, and Edomites. Presence kept David during civil and personal (family) implosions.

The presence of God that was with David, together with the purpose of God for his life, caused God to make a covenant with David that was called in Acts 13:34 "the sure mercies of David." The covenant that God established with David was that He would build his house (his life, family, and kingdom); that He would establish David's son(s) on the throne after him—and that his son, Solomon, would build Him a house for the presence and glory of the Lord to dwell; that he, David, would sit on an eternal throne.

WARNING: DETOUR AHEAD

There had never been a time in David's life where he was without the presence and purpose of God for his life…until one evening when as he was lying on his bed, and made the fateful decision to step out of his bedroom and onto the roof of his house for a bit of fresh air—and to take in the "view."

Have you ever had one of "those" days when you think to yourself, "Maybe I should have just stayed in bed!" I'm pretty sure that at some point in our lives, we have either had this thought or made this statement. I believe that, in hindsight, David must have had this very thought. He would soon live to regret his decision to journey out onto his rooftop that evening. May I offer an observation here? Regret seems to have a way of making us, like David, wish that we had just stayed in bed the day we chose to do what we did that ended up causing us significant amounts of grief.

Sometimes I think that maybe, just maybe, when we are going through difficult situations or making tough decisions, we might do ourselves a bit of a favor to just stay in bed until we have a clear word from the Lord.

If David had only chosen to go to war against the Ammonites with his general, Joab, and the armies of Israel instead of staying home in Jerusalem But he didn't. If only he had not chosen to go outside on that particular evening But he did. The result of these ill-timed decisions was that for the first time in his life, David would come to know what it was to have purpose—but no presence.

A NOT SO TROUBLE-FREE PARADISE

Although his body was at rest as he lay in his bed that evening, David's mind was actively engaged in the movements of his kingdom. He mused over the war with Ammon. I surmise that an internal debate was taking place within him on whether or not he should have gone to battle or if, truly, it was better for him to stay home. His mind was heavy with other things that were taking place outside the walls and borders of his kingdom as well. His thoughts would then shift, turning inward and focusing on things that were taking place within the walls of Jerusalem. It could be that somewhere mixed within these kingdom concerns were thoughts that took him back to the simpler days of his youth when his greatest responsibility was nothing more than fending off a lion or a bear while he led, fed, and watered his flock of sheep. But those days were long behind him, and the pressing needs of a kingdom lay before him and demanded his full attention.

"The roof," he thought. What a perfect place to sit, relax his body and clear his head. Maybe sip some spiced Chai tea with some cookies: spend a little time in prayer, meditating on the Lord and on His promises: just maybe have some quiet time to think things through. It made perfect sense to David. It sounded good, but it wouldn't take long to prove otherwise.

Although the Bible omits this part (and for good reason, I suppose), I can hear in my spirit as David lay on his bed contemplating a relocation to the roof, the Drifters were playing their song 'Up on The Roof' on David's radio as though they were welcoming him to this rooftop encounter.

As David climbed up the stairs that led to the roof of his grand house and the Drifters fading away in the background, David stepped out onto the roof of his palace, his house that had been built for him by God Himself.

Once on the roof, David sat for a while as he drank his tea and ate his cookies. Suddenly, he felt the need to move around a little. He got up and began to pace back and forth, side to side, and looking out over the city of Jerusalem; even with all of its pressures, he thought about how good God had been to him and all the things that He had done in his life.

This time when he thought about where God had brought him from, his thoughts included all those whom he passed over to be positioned where he was; chosen by God to be a king, sitting on a throne in the city of the great God of Israel. Presence and purpose were perfectly positioned and connected for that moment, and he knew it.

It was in this atmosphere that David felt a song begin to well up inside of him. A hymn of praise and thanksgiving that began to rise up from his innermost being like a fresh dug well that had tapped into an inexhaustible reservoir of lyric and tune. A new song was released out of his spirit, and as it ascended up unto the throne of grace, the release of the presence began to overwhelm David, filling his soul with overflowing joy.

"CAN'T TAKE MY EYES OFF YOU"

But as David sang a song of thanksgiving and danced in praise before the Lord, he saw something else out of the corner of his eye that caught his attention. "Whoa!" David thought. "What was that? A woman? What's she doing?" David took a second look, thinking that his eyes might have been playing a trick on him. He moved closer to the edge of his rooftop vantage point just to make sure that he really was seeing what he thought he saw.

"Yep!" 20/20 eyesight. "It's definitely a woman…an unclothed woman. A beautiful woman and she's taking a bath," he said out loud to no one but himself. David's eyes had not lied to him or played a trick on him. He certainly saw a woman, a beautiful woman. The problem was, besides the obvious, this beautiful, naked, bathing woman was also a married woman, but that didn't stop David. He had been bitten and smitten.

The words of David's song of praise and adoration that had flowed so freely as they were drawn up from deep in the well of his heart and released from the fountain of his mouth unto the Lord before he saw Bathsheba began to fail and turned from refreshing words of spirit and truth worship to "You're just too good to be true, can't take my eyes off of you."

With his attention and affection for God now divided, the well of worship was slowly being dammed up and unable to flow like it had when his heart was single toward God: and a new well containing bitter water had been dug and began to spring up within him.

Now, the right thing for our hero to have done would have been to turn himself around, walk across the roof to where the stairs were located, go back to his bedroom, repent, wash his eyes and mind with the water of the Word, and move forward, but that's not exactly how it went down.

MOVING AWAY WHILE MOVING CLOSER

As David moved closer toward Bathsheba in his heart, the presence moved farther away from him, but because his attention and affection had been so completely captivated by what he saw, he did not sense the lifting of the presence as it moved slowly and quietly away from him leaving him only with the emptiness of presence-less purpose.

With his heart breathlessly consumed by the bathing beauty Bathsheba, he was convinced he had to know more about her.

Who was she? Where does she come from? Is she married? David then has the less than brilliant idea to inquire about her. He sends one of his servants to speak to her on his behalf, and upon returning, he tells David that her name is Bathsheba, she is the daughter of Eliam, and she is the WIFE of Uriah, the Hittite. The only thing David heard from his servant is that "her name was Bathsheba, the daughter of blah, blah, blah."

David paid no attention to anything else that was said except her name. If he only had listened with his spirit instead of his lustful soul, he wouldn't have heard anything except that she was married and therefore unapproachable.

Listen, God will never give you another man's wife or another woman's husband.

Had David listened with his spirit, he would have heard his servant tell him that she was the daughter of Eliam, who was the son of David's once trusted counselor, Ahithophel, who conspired with Absalom to overthrow David and kill him. The reason Ahithophel turned on David was because of this very incident.

DINNER AT MY PLACE

David was totally captivated by young Bathsheba. He had to talk to her. He had to know if she was happy just being the wife of an infantryman in the army of Israel, or did she aspire to bigger, better, and brighter things. David extended an invitation to her to have dinner with him, and she accepted it.

Maybe it was David's good looks that caught her off guard; after all, the Bible describes David as being a pretty man. Maybe it was his position or charming personality, or maybe it was his strength and reputation. Maybe she thought no one would ever have to know. After all, her husband was a military man: he was away fighting with the armies of Israel. Maybe she reasoned within herself, 'what if he never makes it back?'

Although doubtful as it may be, maybe it was just the fact that this was the king that pressed her, and she felt that she could not refuse him. Whatever the reason, they spent the evening together "getting to know each other a little better." But before she would leave the palace, the presence had been lifted: they would have an adulterous affair that would prove to be costly as well as deadly.

A THIEF COMES TO KILL, STEAL, AND DESTROY

Adultery must be recognized for what it is: a thief that is out to steal the prosperity of its victims. Prosperity includes money, properties, and other possessions: but it is much more than just tangible things. It also includes physical, mental, emotional, and spiritual health and wealth, but it doesn't stop there. Prosperity is the establishment of character, integrity, stability, structure, success, and godly blessing in the lives of children. Prosperity is peace, rest, joy, wholeness, fullness, security, safety, tranquility, and so much more. Adultery is nothing more than a thief regardless of how it's packaged.

No matter how Javier Hot-lips puckers or Susie Swinging Hips swings it unless you're married to Javier or Susie, you need to leave them alone! If they are trying to separate you from your spouse, they are nothing more than thieves and must be recognized as such.

Jesus said in John 10:10 that a thief has three goals: to kill, to steal, and to destroy. But a thief will not thieve unless they're given an opportunity to. How many lives over centuries of time have been killed, stolen from, and destroyed by such encounters with this thief named adultery.

Adultery has cost couples their marriage, children, emotional as well as physical, mental, and spiritual well-being: It has cost houses, properties, futures, joy, purpose, destinies, and much, much more. Thieves do what they do because they have an evil anointing on them, enabling them to thieve. You cannot allow a thief into your home, nor can you entertain the philosophy of a thief. I am always amazed by people whom I counsel that have allowed thieves to access their lives and then become shocked when they find out they've been thieved. The thief called adultery was no kinder to David and Bathsheba than anyone else that it had infiltrated and deceived. It, like the Lord, is no respecter of person.

Anything that seeks to divide your attention (taking your eyes off of Jesus) and your affection (introducing other lovers than Jesus) is a thief. And if they are not identified as such, and put away, eventually, they will kill, steal, and destroy your life; and will stop at nothing until it has consumed everything of value in it—leaving it in complete ruin.

THE GREAT COVER-UP

One time. That was all it took. Bathsheba became pregnant with David's child, and now David's sin was about to be uncovered. What was done in secret was about to be discovered in the open and declared from the rooftops. Sin will always seek to deceive by causing its victim to believe that somehow they can touch it and it won't come back to them. But sin, after its committed, will immediately turn around and point its finger at the ones who touched it and tell on them. Although Bathsheba went to David's palace and returned home under cover of darkness, the Lord saw everything perfectly as if it were noonday.

Panic struck David upon hearing the news that Bathsheba was pregnant. What they did in secret was about to be openly discovered. The thought of being found out consumed David's mind. Fear, anxiety, and confusion now occupied the place in David's heart where the presence once resided. Isn't that the way sin is, though? It seems so wonderful at the time, but when it's through and it's about to be discovered, its pleasantness turns to panic-driven fear and its taste becomes as bitter as wormwood.

No doubt, David began to think about the implications that could come as a result of this moment of lust-driven absence of wisdom. Panic resulting from sin has a way of making the irrational seem rational. It is capable of clouding logic, reason, and judgment. It makes us believe that we can do the unthinkable and still somehow come out of it all unaffected by its consequence.

David's first plan to cover up his sin was simple enough. He would have Joab send Bathsheba's husband, Uriah, back to Jerusalem to bring him an update on the war. David reasoned within himself that Uriah would go home for a visit with Bathsheba before returning to the front lines, and he would be in the clear. What David didn't realize was that Uriah was a man of strong integrity and a sense of duty. Uriah was summoned to the palace by David, and he waited for him anxiously.

After the king heard the latest news from the frontlines (which at this point he really wasn't concerned about), he encouraged Uriah to go home for a couple of days. He had a wonderful dinner catered for Uriah and Bathsheba so that they could enjoy the evening together. David's thought was that certainly after they wined and dined, a bedroom rendezvous would naturally follow.

Once Uriah left David's presence, the king thought that he could finally sit back and relax with his sin now covered and Bathsheba's honor intact. But what he didn't realize until the morning was that Uriah never went home. His sense of loyalty to his king and to his fellow soldiers would not allow him to go home for some R&R while they were fighting on the battlefield for his king and country. Uriah would sleep on the ground at the king's gate. With the absence of presence, David found himself in a moral and spiritual freefall. With the failure of his first attempt to cover his sin, he became a little more desperate and would have to try a new approach.

"Liquor!" He thought to himself, "If I can get him drunk." After all, people do the craziest things under the influence of alcohol. This time he believed that he would succeed in his plan to hide from the consequences of his choice to ignore what was right before His God and pursue the latest form that the garden's forbidden fruit had taken on.

IT'S NEVER THAT EASY

At this point, David is in a downward spiral that (with each deceptive decision which by their design were made to excuse himself from accountability and cover his sin instead of confronting it and taking responsibility for his actions) spun him uncontrollably faster and faster as it hurled him ever closer toward a disastrous and inevitable encounter with the cruel and unforgiving pavement of disobedience, deception, self-reliance…sin.

The fear of being exposed and labeled as an adulterer, a deceiver, a liar, a hypocrite replaced the place in David that was once occupied by the presence of his God. A stain had appeared on the great king's bright white, starched, and pressed reputation. Taking an unmarried woman as a wife or taking the wife of a man who had passed under less than favorable circumstances was one thing, but this was something altogether different and wrong…and David knew it. This knowledge frightened him beyond his encounters with Saul or the battles that he had fought. The presence was with David then, but now, it had lifted from him.

When David's "plan B" failed, he was at a loss. With the loss of presence came the loss of reason, logic, and moral clarity of judgment. He decided that the only way to solve this unfortunate outcome of his poor judgment, and limit any further collateral damage, was to send Uriah back to the frontline of the battle where the fiercest fighting was taking place. David's final instructions to Joab were "put Uriah in the front and pull back from him," thus ensuring that Uriah would not survive.

When David finished writing Uriah's death sentence, he handed the letter to none other than Uriah himself, who faithfully carried the letter signed and sealed by the king himself, and he delivered it to Joab. Upon reading the letter, I can only imagine what must have been going on in Joab's mind at this point.

He had no idea of the king's motivation for writing it, but being the loyal general that he was and David's close friend, unquestioningly, he did as David instructed. He followed every command. And when the inevitable happened, and Uriah was slain, Joab sent word back to David confirming that the deed had been done.

ENQUIRING MINDS WANT TO KNOW

As hard as David tried to keep this out of the tabloids of his day, his sin found him out. What was done in secret was now being proclaimed from the rooftops. Although it was done under the cover of darkness, God had seen it from the beginning, and it wasn't long before Bathsheba's father, grandfather, members of David's army, family, and others in Jerusalem had found out what he had done.

DAVID'S TRIP TO GOD'S WOODSHED

When my boys were young, they would, from time to time, engage in "unacceptable behavior" that would require a trip to the woodshed for an "adjustment," Over the years, not unlike myself growing up, they would become very familiar with the inside décor of the woodshed. I made it a practice never to correct or make "adjustments" in my boy's behavior or attitude when I was angry with them. I never wanted them to confuse correction with abuse. I would always wait until I could correct them, motivated out of love for them and not anger toward them. Prior to making the appropriate adjustment that was needed, I would always tell them to go into my bedroom and wait on me.

I would explain to them what was acceptable and unacceptable. I would explain to them what the Bible said about it and why I needed to correct them. With that said, then, I would make the adjustment. When I had finished, I would tell them to put their arms around my neck, hug me, and tell me that they loved me: and I would hug them and tell them how much I loved them, and it was my love for them that provoked me to discipline them.

Solomon says that only a parent that hates their children don't discipline them. They would put their arms around me, and I would listen as they whispered four words that made my heart melt every time "I love you, dad," and I would reply, "I love you too, son."

When David made his decision to go out onto the roof that day, I am confident that he had no idea of its price tag. He was completely unaware of the coming choices that he would be forced to make, and what he would ultimately choose was going to cost him the presence of God that had always accompanied his purpose, and this would only be the beginning. He would soon learn firsthand that sin would not be satisfied until it bankrupts the lives of men and women. The presence was the greatest forfeiture, but it didn't stop there. The cost was so much more than the presence. It cost him friendship's, alliances, a wise and trusted counselor, two sons, loyal military leaders and soldiers, his reputation, a woodshed encounter with God where He would choose the switch that was to be used, and finally, it almost cost him the kingdom as well as his life. Woodshed experiences are never pleasant, but they are always necessary. When the woodshed door finally opened, and David, having composed himself, put his arms around the neck of the Lord and whispered in his ear, "I love you Father," and his Father hugged him in return and whispered back, "I love you too, son."

COMING OUT A BETTER MAN

David emerged from the Lord's whipping shed bruised, broken, and humbled. But he also came out of that shed forgiven, restored, and determined. If you were to look closely, you would have seen that David went into that shed alone, but he didn't come out of it alone: he came out of it with the presence once again holding his hand.

When the presence of God became reunited with the purpose of David, the chase was on again. The Lord and David picked up the chase from they left off. Now it would be a lifelong, undistracted pursuit by a king who was after the heart of the King.

Chapter Eight

~~~~~~~~~~

Digested or Vomited?

ALMOST FROM BEGINNING TO END, life is filled with questions. Some questions are very important, and some, not so much; but they are questions nonetheless that either will be or must be answered. When I think of questions that are asked and answered, one comes to mind that most people never ask under these terms, but this is a very valid question and, at some point, in just about every person's life, it, in some form or another, will be asked and will be answered whether the person recognizes it as such or not.

The question is simply this: Give your choice of the two; would you rather be digested or vomited? Now, while neither of these options sounds ideal or pleasant, people make the choice every day through their thoughts and actions that determine whether they will be digested or vomited.

I am sure that, at least to some degree, most of us know the story of Jonah: and how that purpose without presence caused him to be faced with this very question in a real and tangible way that probably none of us will ever know or experience in any other way except through the imaginations and imagery of our minds and thoughts: and I believe that I speak for all of us when I say, for that, we are grateful.

Many of us become familiar with the story of Jonah at a very early age from Sunday school teachings or dramatic reenactments, etc. But I believe that the story of Jonah is anything but elementary or something that should be reenacted on an elementary level.

The lessons that we receive from his story are far too valuable to leave to the understanding of the junior's classes or to stereotypical low-budget church productions. The truths and principles that we find in the story of Jonah are far too deep for that.

Now, having said that, we will have a little fun at the Prophet Jonah's expense, but ultimately, I want you to see how that Jonah's purpose without presence got him into a place that, even in his wildest imagination, he never could have thought up or seen coming.

Ch1:1 of the Book of Jonah reads like this "Now the Word of the Lord came unto Jonah." Although there is a little more to this verse, I want to stop right there because I believe that if God takes the time to send us His Word, we ought to take some time to read it, understand it, and do what He said. Often easier said than done, isn't it?

The Lord had come to Jonah with a Word, not for the Prophet, but for the people of the city of Nineveh. The Word was as short as it was direct: "Arise, go to Nineveh, that great city, and cry out against it: for their wickedness has come up before Me."

At this point, Jonah had purpose, and he had presence; what he lacked was the willingness to be obedient to the commission of God. When Jonah heard the Word of the Lord, he immediately began to pack his suitcase with the things that he would need for such a journey. The problem was that his destination and the Lord's destination were a paltry twenty-two hundred miles or so in opposite directions.

Instead of going to Nineveh, Jonah chose to go down to the cruise ship terminal and buy a one-way ticket on a ship that was bound for some sun and fun. In packing his suitcase full, Jonah gave an appearance of obedience: after all, no one was watching him pack that suitcase...no one would ever have a reason to question its contents, right?? What Jonah had not factored into his great plan to escape the commission was that as he packed, he packed in plain view of the one who had given the commission.

Instead of Jonah's suitcase being filled with the things he would need to fulfill the purpose of God, he filled it with the things that he would need for his vacation. After all, he was going to a coastal city in Western Spain and would be lying in a hammock on a sun-soaked beach while sipping one of those fruit drinks in a coconut cup with a little umbrella on the top. In his mind's eye, he could already see himself on that beach, in that hammock, with that drink in hand. He pictured himself sipping that fruit drink slowly and savoring every drop: all the while watching the little umbrella as it was being twirled ever so gently by a warm ocean breeze. He packed a couple of Hawaiian print shirts, tank-tops, cargo shorts, flip-flops, a straw hat, some suntan lotion, and a Hebrew/Spanish dictionary that was complete with the most common Spanish phrases that would enable him to get directions, book a hotel, and order from restaurant menus once he had arrived.

With suitcase in hand and wearing the disguise of a tourist (so as not to be discovered as a disobedient prophet), he set off for the cruise ship terminal. He had concocted a foolproof plan, or so he thought. What Jonah failed to realize was that even though he wore a disguise, the Lord knew who he was, what he had packed, where he was going, where he should be going, and what he should have been doing. The Lord knew it all.

THE MASQUERADE

Several years ago, Val and I received an invitation to attend a masquerade party. Everyone was wearing colorful and expressive masks. The premise behind wearing the mask is so that the wearer can hide their true identity and take on the identity of the mask, which supposedly released them from the responsibility for their actions; after all, it wasn't the person behind the mask, it was the mask itself that influenced their behavior.

The problem with that is, at least at this masquerade, everyone knew who the person behind the mask was. God is the same way, isn't He? We try our hardest to wear disguises or masks that we hope will hide our identity, hide who we really are: but just as we were able to recognize the identity of every person behind the mask, God is able to recognize us as well.

In this, I realize that no matter the disguises that we wear (and from time to time, we've all worn them) that give a different appearance on the outside than what is on the inside and are capable of fooling those whose view is limited to the outside; they are still worthless before God. We've all worn disguises that enabled us to blend in with our surroundings, but the disguise wasn't really who we are or what we are.

I call this masquerade *"Chameleon Christianity."* A *Chameleon Christian* is a Christian that changes their appearance to blend in with whatever environment they find themselves in. Like some people in the Church today, Jonah was a classic example of Chameleon Christianity. In fact, I think that maybe he could have been known as the father of *Chameleon Christianity!* Unfortunately, fooling others really doesn't have much value, does it? And although we know this: many times, and for many self-justifiable reasons, we still do it, don't we?

God is the only One that matters, and He is able to look beyond, and if you will, through the disguises and masks that we wear and see the inside. He knows who and what we really are; no matter what we try to make other people believe that we really are. Can I make a suggestion? Take off the disguise. The only one that really matters has already accepted you just as you are, but having said that, He loves you too much to leave you the way you are. His desire is to change you through the power of His Word and indwelling Sprit into the image of His Son, Jesus.

ONE, PLEASE

I can see Jonah as he went up to the ticket booth, looking this way and that way, making sure that he was not recognized by anyone that might question what he was doing, where he was going, or why he was dressed the way he was. He looked around but saw no one: and yet he still had this strange feeling that he couldn't shake. No matter how hard he tried, he couldn't help but feel that someone had followed him and that someone was still watching him. Purpose without presence was about to take Jonah on a trip that would end up costing him a whole lot more than the price of admission.

After buying his ticket, clinching the handle of his suitcase tightly, and with his stomach sorely in a knot, Jonah climbed up the ramp and onto the deck of the ship and went down to the ship's cafeteria to get a ginger ale and relax. After ordering his drink and hoping that it would calm his stomach, he slipped into a dark corner booth and sunk down in it. He wondered if he had made a clean get-a-way. As the ship left the port and began to set sail, he was finally starting to calm down. He even felt a small sense of relief that his plan, to this point, seemed to be working flawlessly. The knot in his stomach began un unwrap itself. Because of all the stress of executing his plan, he was mentally, emotionally, and physically exhausted. He became overwhelmed by the need to sleep. "Just for a moment," he said in a voice barely above a whisper to himself. Then he drifted off to sleep.

Unknowingly to Jonah, God had boarded that same ship. Even though he wasn't wearing a disguise, He slipped in behind Jonah and had followed him on deck and then down to the cafeteria. He sat down at a booth adjacent to Jonah's and watched him as he slept. Jonah was too sleepy to notice that God was sitting across from him, and that He was watching Jonah's every move.

JEALOUSY IS A TWO-EDGED SWORD

The Bible says in Exodus 20:5, Ex.34:14, Deut.4:24, 5:9, 6:15, Josh.24:19, and Nahum 1:2 that God is a jealous God. The jealousy that God has for people is like a two-edged sword. It provokes Him to mercy as well as justice. The jealousy of God for the people of Nineveh commissioned Jonah to go there and preach to the people a message of repentance. Upon their acceptance of His mercy, His jealousy released the blessing connected to repentance. On the other hand, His jealousy also provoked Him to judge Jonah for his disobedience. We must understand the jealousy of God works the same way in the world today, as well as in our own lives.

It was the jealousy of God that provoked Him to send Jesus to die for our sins. It was His jealousy that emplaced the covenant of grace and all that it contains. When we repent of our sins, it is His jealousy that releases forgiveness and imparts the fullness of Kingdom blessings. But on the other side, it is also His jealousy that provokes justice and judgment on those who refuse to accept this grace through disobedience and rebelliousness, including those who belong to Him but are walking in disobedience and rebellion. The Book of Nahum is a perfect example of this.

WARNING: DISOBEDIENCE CAN CAUSE LONG TERM VISION AND HEARING LOSS

A while ago, I was reading in Ezek.12. As I read verse 2, God spoke something into my spirit that I will never forget. Verse 2 reads, "Son of man, you dwell in the midst of a rebellious house, which has eyes, but can't see; and has ears, but can't hear—because, they are rebellious.'

When I read that, the Lord spoke to me and said, 'Rebellion is the leading cause of spiritual blindness and deafness in the Church today.' He said that it was like someone who once had sight but lost it, and now their sight consists of nothing more than mental imagery of order and placement of things that were. Also, it is like someone who at one time could hear, but for whatever reason, they are no longer capable of hearing sounds. So, the sounds they hear are nothing more than sounds they heard that have been stored in their memory. They live in what they saw and what they heard—instead of what they see and what they hear.

KARAOKE NIGHT!

With the first day at sea passed, while feeling more relaxed, as well as finally getting his sea legs, Jonah began to tour the ship. He read a banner on the ship's entertainment schedule that read "Tonight is Karaoke Night." O, how Jonah loved to sing! He knew all of the classics of his day. "Karaoke!" he thought. This was just what he needed to help him finish unwinding and have some fun at the same time. That evening, Jonah came to the ship's lounge where the good times were about to roll. After all, who doesn't like Karaoke night! Jonah went to the ship's DJ and got the book containing all of the songs that he could choose from. The first song his eyes fell on was a familiar song to him but was totally out of place for his environment. The song's title, "I surrender all." Jonah must have thought that his eyes must have been playing a trick on him, but just in case they weren't, without looking down again, he quickly turned to another page. He read the title of the next song he saw and knew this would be the one that he would bring down the house with, literally. "My way!" he thought. "I did it my way!" There he was now, standing on the stage, illuminated by the spotlight. The DJ started the song, and Jonah, summoning his inner Elvis, out of his mouth and right on cue came the very familiar words of a very familiar song that many of us who have been in Jonah's current position have also sung. The finale! Jonah, down on one knee and his head bowed. With the microphone in his left hand and his right hand extended in glorious triumph, Jonah sang the last line of the infamous song that testified of his decision to disobey the Lord. He belted out the words in classic Elvis style, "And did it my.... waaaaaaaaaay!"

The lounge erupted in thunderous applause from the ship's other passengers as well as its crew. Never had they heard such conviction, such defiance, such determination, and such passion in a Karaoke performance. What they didn't realize was that Jonah had not sung this song for their entertainment; no, that would have been easy. Jonah sung this song for the one passenger that no one saw board the ship, the one that no one saw in the cafeteria, and no one saw sitting at what appeared to be an empty table right in front of center stage: however it may have appeared to be, the table was anything but unoccupied.' There was one chair and one occupant. Unlike everyone else who accompanied Jonah on his disobedient excursion, He wasn't cheering or applauding. He sat there quietly with His arms folded. He didn't have anything to say because His expression said everything.

They hadn't been at sea for too long, three days to be exact, before the shipmen began to notice a slight change in the weather. They noticed that the wind had picked up a little, and the sea was getting a little choppier. They saw it off in the distance—a wall of large, dark, ominous clouds heading directly toward them. They stood in fear as they watched the ferocity of the lightning as massive bolts flashed in all directions through the clouds. Now, it was getting so close that they not only could hear the boom of the thunder, but they could feel it as well as it shook the entire ship. First the lightning, then seconds later, an ear-piercing crack of thunder that began to violently shake the ship and its passengers. They found themselves in the middle of what Jonah 1:4 calls "a mighty tempest." In fact, the storm was so powerful that within minutes of entering its grip, fissures began to compromise the structural integrity of the ship.

All of the shipmen and all the passengers (except for one) were on deck, pulling out their rabbits' feet, lucky coins, crosses, statues, and everything else that they thought might bring them luck—and were crying out to every god they could think of to help them. And at the same time, they were also putting on life jackets. They began throwing out the ship's cargo. Everything that could be tossed was thrown over the railing and into the violently churning waters of the great Mediterranean Sea.

THE TRUE COST OF DISOBEDIENCE

We are mistaken if we believe that the consequence of disobedience only affects the disobedient. Over my years in ministry, I have heard people say things like this when they do what they know is either unproductive or counter-productive for their lives, "Besides," they say, "I'm not hurting anyone but myself." First of all, that right there should be incentive enough not to want to do dumb stuff. (Remember: jealous for yourself and jealous for your future with a godly jealousy). Second, they could not be more wrong. Everything we do, right or wrong, good or bad, affects someone besides us. The Apostle Paul said in Rom.14:7 that no man lives unto himself, and no man dies unto himself. What this means is that everything we do affects somebody either in a positive way or a negative way. We were never created to be 'islands' unto ourselves, even though this is what Jonah set off searching for and hoping to find.

Think about this. Everyone in relation to Jonah and that ship lost something of great value. The merchants whose products had been loaded on that vessel were to be sold in the region. Jonah's disobedience not only cost them their merchandise, but it also cost them the profit they would have made as it was sold and distributed. Jonah's disobedience cost the other passengers all of their belongings. It all but cost the captain his ship. And it almost cost them all their lives…including Jonah.

There are things that belong to our prosperity and the prosperity of others that are sacrificed through the storms that come as a result of disobedience and rebellion. I believe that King Manasseh of Judah, if he were reading this, would surely give me an "Amen" right about now because if there was one person who could testify about the high price of rebellion and disobedience, it was him.

2Chron.33 talks about him and how he was made king over Judah in place of his father, Hezekiah. Unlike his father, Manasseh was a wicked young man, and the Bible says that he did evil in the sight of the Lord. As you read through Ch.33, you would see a laundry list of ungodly practices and policies that Manasseh had put in place; including the sacrificing of his own children to the idol god, Molech. I won't get into all the horrible things that Manasseh did, but if you're curious, you can check it out for yourself (2Chron.33 the entire chapter).

The one thing that I will say is that Manasseh came to the place where he repented of his evil acts, and the Lord, in His mercy, forgave him and reestablished him of the throne in Judah—but the children that he sacrificed were never recovered. And neither were the things that were tossed over the side of the ship Jonah was on.

We cannot afford to be deceived by the lie that says disobedience only affects the disobedient. Everything we do will have an effect on someone. There are people whose eternal prosperity is counting on you to be obedient to God. With the merchandise gone, and the possessions of the passengers gone, there would be nothing left to do but to try and salvage the ship they were all on together. You might even say that "they were all in the same boat!" Sorry. Disobedience always leaves the disobedient and all who are in relation to them emptied, battered, broken, and salvaged.

THE SLEEPING PROPHET

Okay. Not all of the passengers were on the deck fighting to save the ship and, in the process, their own lives as well. The Bible says that Jonah was still in his bunk with the covers pulled up over his head, fast asleep. The previous night's Karaoke performance had worn Jonah out, and now, all he wanted to do was sleep.

Have you ever wondered how in the world Jonah could have slept through all of this? I mean, with the noise of the storm, the to and fro tossing of the ship by the wind and waves: not to mention the ship's captain barking out orders to shipmen and passengers alike. It was total pandemonium on the ship's deck. The people spent their whole time running aimlessly around the deck. If you don't know what you're doing, sometimes you can appear to if you can stay moving, I guess. I believe that the depth of Jonah's physical slumber testified to the slumber that his spirit had been overcome by through his disobedience. It is amazing the depth of spiritual slumber that purpose without presence can cause.

God said to the Prophet Isaiah in Ch.6:10 that because of Israel's disobedience, He would cause the ears of the people to become heavy and their eyes sleepy, both of which are depictions of the dull grogginess that accompanies a deep sleeping person.

With the storm raging and still needing to lighten the ship in hopes of stabilizing it so that it would not sink, the captain went down into the interior of the ship. He was looking for something, anything that he could carry back up and toss overboard. As he entered the passengers' cabin area looking for expendables that he could send up and over, he looked and saw Jonah. His eyes were darting around the room so quickly that he almost looked right over him as he lay sleeping in his bunk. In total disbelief, the captain forced his way forward into Jonah's room and toward his bed. Jonah was still in his Hawaiian shirt, tank-top, and cargo shorts. The captain grabbed hold of Jonah and began to shake him with a force that the storm could not compare to.

As he is shaking Jonah, the captain screams, "Wake Up! How can you sleep at a time like this!?" Jonah was now trying to wake up and, in the process, clear the fog that had rolled into his mind preventing him from understanding the gravity of their situation. Soon he would understand the circumstances that had created their fear and sense of urgency.

The shipmaster, as he is called, tells Jonah to pray. "Pray?" Jonah thought to himself. Prayer was the last thing on his mind at this point. He already knew exactly what was going on and why. He knew that even though he hadn't seen Him board the ship with him in Joppa: Jonah knew the Lord was on that ship. He had been there all the time, and now, Jonah knew it. Pray? Jonah knew he had no need to pray. He knew that all of this was his fault; all of it had been caused by his disobedience. He knew the storm and the loss of the ship's cargo were the result of purpose disconnected from the presence. When Jonah bought that one-way ticket to Tarshish, the presence lifted and presence-less purpose produced a devastating storm with a high price tag.

THE TOURIST EXPOSED

I can see all the ship's crew and passengers as they rock, paper, and scissored their way to find out who the offender was that caused this storm and the trouble that came with it. Jonah may have been going down, but he wasn't going down without a fight. When it came down to two, Jonah threw paper and the other guy threw scissors. Jonah was the guilty man. He knew it, and now, they knew it. When at last his disguise had been completely blown away by the wind of God's will, the crew of the ship pleaded with him to know who he was and what he had done that caused this great catastrophe and loss. They asked him four questions, with probably the most important one being the first. 1. They asked Jonah what his occupation was. 2. They asked him where he was coming from. 3. They asked him where he was born. 4. They asked him what his nationality was.

Knowing that he had been discovered: his straw hat having been blown off of his head and into the sea; his sunglasses had fallen from the neck of his tank-top in all the ruckus and had been stepped on; and his shirt and shorts in shreds—and who knows where his flip-flops went: maybe it was time for Jonah to come clean. Jonah proceeds to answer their questions. He tells them who he is and whose he is; he tells them about the God he served and His awesome and fearful capabilities: and when he finishes, the sailors were far more afraid of Jonah's God than they were of the storm He sent.

Naturally, their next question would have been a logical one by anyone's standards. They asked him, "You serve a God like that! What were you even thinking?"

The seasoned sailors were afraid, and rightly so because they too knew that Jonah might have appeared to be alone as he bought that ticket in Joppa and boarded that ship bound for Tarshish, but they were now convinced that even though they didn't see Him board the ship, they knew He was on it.

They also knew that the cause of this great tempest was because Jonah had disobediently fled from the commission of the Lord. The voice of disobedience can only keep quiet for so long, and then, right on cue, and at the most inopportune time, it will sing an accusation against the disobedient like a stool pigeon. It will lure you, deceive you, entrap you, tell on you, and then mock your calamity.

THE PLAN

What to do? What to do? That's the question. What to do? They began to look for options. They asked Jonah, since he was well acquainted with this God that was able to move nature at will, what would it take for Him to calm the storm? The answer was simple, really.

Over the years, Val and I have counseled many couples who were facing issues and challenges related to the subject of marriage. I have a saying that I use a lot in counseling, and it goes like this: everything is easy until we choose to complicate it. There are easy answers to just about everything we face, no matter what it relates to. The problem comes when we either don't like the answer, or we complicate it with things like "but" or "I can't" or "you don't know," etc. These things can cloud and complicate solutions to problems that otherwise could be fairly easily resolved.

As I said in a previous chapter, Val and I have been married for several decades now, and the thing I point to and credit for our success in marriage is the fact that we have chosen to take the Word of God as the final authority for our lives and our marriage. If what we thought or wanted to do or felt that we had a right to do didn't measure up to the standard of what God said…we set our words, feelings, and rights aside, and we embraced the Lord's because His Word is always right. The result of this has been that after more than four decades of marriage, we still love each other: we even still like each other. We are still best friends.

Yes. There are easy solutions to every problem we face: we may not always like the answer, but I have found that it is usually the easiest answer that is the best one to fix the problem. Many times, we don't like the easy answer because it costs us personally. The easy answer may cause us to have to humble ourselves, or forgive, or admit, and these things have a tendency to make us want to look for other options, and it is here that complications usually enter. I say, keep it easy.

Jonah's easy solution was to toss him overboard. He told the men that if they would pick him up and throw him over the rail and into the sea, the wind and waves would cease, and the calm that they so desperately desired would be obtained. The problem that brought the complication to this easy solution was these men's consciences. Their conscience wouldn't allow them to pick Jonah up like an archaically barbarous mob and throw him into the sea without feeling that his death would be on their hands. They were too cultured for that. Their solution was to put their backs to it and row harder, but they found it impossible to row against the presence of God and the purpose of God for Jonah's life.

"HATE TO SEE YOU GO…BUT, ADIOS!"

By now, these men had been fighting the storm for several hours. They were physically, mentally, and emotionally exhausted. They had come to the end of themselves and their ability. After having said a prayer: the contents of which was a plea for their own lives and to be forgiven for what they were about to do, with one accord, they picked up Jonah and tossed him over the rail and into the sea with all their might.

What these sailors didn't realize was that God had everything under control. Jonah was in the air between the boat and the water, and before he could think about sticking his landing, a great fish jumped up from the sea and swallowed the Prophet and would-be (if God had only left him alone) tourist.

I believe that it was also at this point that Jonah had an epiphany. "Maybe, just maybe," he thought as he was in mid-air, "Maybe, I should have just gone to Nineveh in the first place! Maybe I wouldn't be in this situation; maybe, I wouldn't be about to fall into the mouth of this huge fish!" If it now could have only been that easy!

Purpose without presence resulting from disobedience will never let you off that easy. There is a price to be paid, and it will be paid in full.

As soon as Jonah was safely tucked away in the fish's belly, the clouds disseminated, the wind calmed, and the waves ceased. Then another fear had come to these seamen, they feared the Lord God of Jonah, and they offered sacrifices to Him and made a vow to make Him their God. Although Scripture doesn't record it, I almost believe that from that time on, all future passengers on that ship were subject to what was known as *"Jonah's Law,"* which involved a security screening to ensure there would be no Jonah type issues before they were allowed to board the ship for travel.

THE JOURNEY BACK TO THE BEGINNING

Immediately after swallowing Jonah, the fish made an abrupt U-turn and set a course for the place where Jonah was when he boarded the ship, thinking that he had made an undetected and successful escape. The journey back to where it all began would take the same amount of time to get back as it took to go out…three days and three nights.

Purpose without presence had taken the Prophet on a journey that he wished to God he had never gone on. Jonah's purpose never left him. The Lord never said to him, "That's okay, Jonah! You go on and enjoy yourself. We can do this another time. Or, maybe I can get someone else to do it. No worries!" Jonah's purpose was still there, and although the presence was not, it was moving back toward the Prophet to see if maybe now he was ready to revisit the commission that had been given to him a few days earlier.

TODAY, I SET BEFORE YOU; DIGESTED OR VOMITED: CHOOSE TO BE VOMITED

Now, Jonah finds himself in the fish's belly, and it's not quite as comfortable as the cabin he was staying in on the ship. It smelled horrible. There were decaying pieces of fish floating around him as well as seaweed and other things that were too decomposed to recognize. The lining of the fish's stomach was rubbing all over Jonah's head and body. The acids contained in the fish's stomach began to bleach Jonah's skin and caused him to start losing his hair. It was nearly impossible to breathe.

It was at this point Jonah had to ask himself one of life's more significant and consequential questions: Would I rather be digested or vomited? God had given him a choice. These were his only options. They are also the only options for all who find themselves in their personal "fish's belly" due to disobedience that, like Jonah, left them with purpose but without presence. Don't be fooled. The presence will not cohabitate with disobedience; the one is sacrificed of the other.

Chapter 2:1 says that Jonah prayed unto the Lord. And although verse two says that the Lord heard his prayer in the fish's belly, it seems to me that the words which Samuel the Prophet spoke concerning Saul in 1Samuel 15:22, where he said "To obey is better than sacrifice" are applicable here.

Had Jonah only obeyed the Lord's commission, none of this would have happened to him in the first place. He would have retained the presence and his purpose. The ship, its cargo, its passengers, and its crew would have had a profitable journey and outcome. And most important to Jonah, he would not be in the Lord's concept of a submarine experiencing all of its unpleasant odors and foul contents. In his prayer of repentance, Jonah chose to be vomited over being digested.

It must have been divine providence that enabled Jonah to survive the three-day journey back to Joppa. There are some who believe that Jonah actually died on the journey and that the Lord gave him back his life upon his exodus from the fish's belly. I don't know. But this I do know, the same God that prepared that fish to swallow him also prepared a way for him to survive.

If you ever find yourself in your own fish's belly, be encouraged. When you call out to the Lord in repentance, the same God that prepared it for you will be the same God who will keep you through it and deliver you from it when you choose to be vomited. Kind of gross, I know. Apologies made.

The fish had just about reached its destination. If the fish had been equipped with a para-scope, Jonah would have been able to see that the city of Joppa was now in view, and it wouldn't be long until he could leave his less than hospitable host; and Jonah's vacation nightmare would finally come to an end.

The fish was racing toward the shore and headed for the perfect place on the beach to deposit its passenger. It came up out of the water and, having done its best Shamu impersonation, it literally threw up Jonah, tossing him up onto the sand: and then it shimmied its way backward into the water and disappeared into the dark waters of the Mediterranean Sea. Jonah lay there on the beach. He felt the sand. He thought that maybe this would have been how the sand on one of those beaches in Tarshish might have felt—had he actually made it to Tarshish: and although he was not exactly sure where he was, he knew he wasn't in Spain. He knew there would be no hammock, no warm ocean breezes, no fruit drinks in coconut cups with little umbrellas. It took him a few minutes to get his bearings. After all, he had just spent the last three days in a fish's belly, heading away from somewhere he wanted to be.

As he sat there on the beach, he lifted up his hands and saw them as well as his whole body covered in the stench and slime of stomach fluid. He wanted to go rinse himself in the sea, but understandably he was a little apprehensive. His skin was bleached and most of his hair gone. Can you imagine what the beachgoers in Joppa must have thought when they saw him? I kind of think that Jonah looked for a creek or an oasis or something besides the sea to clean himself, and I can't say that I blame him.

ON TO NINEVEH! O, YAY...

Joppa was about seven hundred miles or so west of Nineveh. Jonah made his way from Joppa through the rugged terrain of the mountains and the blazing heat of the desert. Nothing of this journey was comfortable. Not the cruise, not the submarine ride, nor the journey from Joppa to Nineveh. It was hard, hot, and miserable. No wonder Jonah had a bad attitude! He obviously didn't travel well. I have been on mission trips with people who don't travel well and, let me tell you, it's a barrel of monkeys! And as we know, there's nothing more fun than a barrel of monkeys...or so they say (Sarcasm mine). Jonah was one of those missionaries that didn't travel well.

The Apostle Paul learned this all too well when he, Barnabas, and Barnabas' nephew, John Mark, went on a mission trip together and, for whatever reason, John Mark left the team and returned home. I kind of think that he didn't travel well either, and it caused some contention between Paul and Barnabas.

That experience stuck so deeply in Paul that he refused to allow him to go on any future trips. When he tried to join the team, Paul said emphatically, No.

STRENGTH FOR THE JOURNEY

Every step that Jonah took toward Nineveh brought the presence of God closer to the Prophet. With the presence came the renewed commission, and it encouraged Jonah to press on, focused forward, until he reached his destination and delivered his message.

Well, we know what happened from here. Jonah finally entered Nineveh and fulfilled the commission. He preached the message of repentance, and the people got saved. Choruses of 'O Happy Day' began to ring out in the streets of Nineveh. Everyone was singing; well, everyone except Jonah. Who knows why Jonah was such a grumpy prophet? I'm always amazed at how God could take a grumpy, whiny, disobedient person like Jonah and use him so greatly: but then there are times I find when I look into the mirror, and I see my reflection staring back at me, and I have to thank God for His great mercy and grace.

WWYD?

What would you do? Jonah chose to be vomited. Let me ask you who, like Jonah, are running in the opposite direction from your call and commission.

Would you rather be digested or vomited? How about neither? How about staying positioned in obedience and avoiding the fish's belly altogether?

There are three options that can be chosen, and the power to choose is yours. First, you can choose to be digested. Many throughout the years have chosen this route, but I wouldn't suggest it.

Being digested is defined as having presence and purpose but either you lost the presence and never recovered it, or you never allowed His presence to connect with your purpose in the first place. The Bible is filled with examples of those who chose to be digested, such as Cain, Esau, Saul, Judas, and Demas, just to name a few.

The second option is to be vomited, which is better than being digested. Jonah chose this option. He said in Ch2:9, "I will pay my vows." He declared that his salvation was only from the Lord.

Paraphrased, Jonah said that being vomited is of the Lord. How do we know this is from the Lord? Jonah 2:10 says that He spoke to the fish, and it vomited Jonah on the sand.

Being vomited is defined as having the Lord's presence connected to our purpose, but for whatever reason, we choose not to walk in or comply with the Lord's purpose; and for a season, our purpose gets disconnected from His presence. But, when we return to Him, His presence reunites us with our purpose, and we are able to complete all that He has called us to do. The Bible is filled with examples of this as well, such as Jonah, David, Moses, Abraham, Sarah, and the Apostle Peter...just to name a few.

I have an observation I would like to make here. Being vomited is better than being digested. In times where we are found in disobedience, it is not the Lord's will for us to be digested and consumed, but that we would be released from the vehicle that He uses to bring us back unto Himself.

The third choice is to avoid the first two! We don't have to be consumed or brought back—how about if we never leave? How about if we keep our purpose connected with His presence through obedience, by doing what the Lord said to do?

We can choose what we want; that power is in our control. But remember, we, as the chooser, will always serve our choice. Might I encourage us to choose wisely.

Chapter Nine

---◦◦◦---

Preparing for the presence

IMAGINE FOR A MOMENT THAT you had received an invitation from the Queen of England to come to the Buckingham Palace for tea and biscuits. You can be sure that contained in the invitation would be a list that no doubt would detail things you would be required to do, such as being punctual, wearing proper attire, maintaining the correct posture, and her majesty's social preferences. You would be instructed on proper etiquette: how you should walk, talk, act, and present yourself to her. Contained in this invitation would also be a list of "do's" as well as "don'ts." The "don'ts' are things that would be offensive or out of order, such as showing up to the palace in shorts, a tank-top, and flip-flops and using ill-mannered behavior.

If the code or protocol was not adhered to, the likelihood of you being entertained by the Queen would not be very good. The instructions concerning protocol would be there in the invitation so that you would understand that you can't just go waltzing into the Queen's presence any way you decide to do so. There is an expectation that if you accept the invite and have an audience with the Queen, you must read, understand, apply, and comply with all the rules defining proper protocol.

If this is true with the royalty of earth, why would we think that it would not be true with the Royalty of Heaven, the King of Glory, The Almighty God! Protocol for entering the presence of earthy dignitaries alludes to the fact that there is protocol for entering the presence of the King of kings. The earthly is a mirror that reflects this, and testifies of it. There is protocol for entrance to and obtaining an audience with the Creator of heaven, earth, and all things contained within them.

Just as it is unacceptable to come into the presence of the Queen unannounced, ill-prepared, or according to our own terms or design, it is more so unacceptable to come into the presence of the very God without meeting all the requirements that protocol demands for entrance into the throne room filled with His presence and majesty.

If there is one Book in the Bible that illustrates this, defines it for us, and teaches us concerning the proper protocol for entering into and possessing the presence and connecting to our purpose, it is the Book of Esther.

The Book of Esther is a story about a young Jewish girl whose Hebrew name was Hadassah, but was later changed to the Persian, Esther, meaning Star—and a Media-Persian King.

NO SUCH THING AS RESPONSIBLE DRINKING.

As the story goes, King Ahasuerus one day decided that he was going to make a feast for the nobility of the Medo-Persian Empire, its princes…and servants. The king took the royal guests around the kingdom and showed them all of its glory and wealth for one hundred and eighty days. At the end of the tour, the king decided that he was going to make this feast a week-long event. He even decided to invite some of the common people that lived in the city of Shushan where the king's palace was located to join with him in the festivities.

The royal party organizers had done an exceptional job of designing and decorating the royal garden. The way that it is described in the first chapter of the Book of Esther suggests that it must have been truly an awesome sight to behold. No corners were cut, no expense was spared. The feast came complete with an open bar. This was sure to be a state department feast that would, for better or worse, be remembered and talked about for years, even centuries, to come.

Now, Ahasuerus' feast was kind of a 'golf' feast. It was a 'gentlemen only, ladies forbidden' affair. And so, not to outdone by her husband, Ahasuerus' wife, Queen Vashti, made a feast for the noble women as well as some of the common women who lived in Shushan.

At the end of the seventh day, after much wine and who knows what else had been consumed, the king commanded his closest servants to go and call Vashti, the Queen, to come and present herself before the king as well as his guests. The reason? The Bible says that Vashti was "fair" to look upon, that means that she was very beautiful from head to toe. She, like the glories of the Medo-Persian kingdom, was a symbol of Ahasuerus' conquest, power, and position.

I've often wondered what would possess a man to want to parade his wife before a group of men. Being a man, I know how men are! Especially when those men have hearts 'merry with wine.' These men, after drinking wine for seven days straight, were all drunk. I can only imagine what that whole environment must have been like. Wine can make a wise man foolish, it can make a powerful man weak, and it can make a married man single.

THE TROUBLE WITH UPPITY WOMEN.

By the answer that Vashti had given, which consisted of something along the lines of "I don't think so, pal!', she was not as "merry in heart" as her husband was. She said "Go tell the king for me "that's an idea...not a very good one...but it is an idea!" She had no intention of allowing herself to be paraded before this throng of intoxicated men, and the king should have never placed her in the position. But that's wine for you!

Well, as you can imagine, that didn't sit well with the king, and his wine-induced 'merry heart' turned into a humiliated and totally embarrassed heart, which manifested itself as a raging one. Alcohol can do that to a person. For a season, it can take a happy man and make him happier, but it can also take an angry man and make him angrier. Yes, it can make a fool of the wise and reduce a fool to dust—but the end result of all of them is the same. Alcohol bites like a serpent and stings like an adder. It skews vision, understanding, and morality. It is the source of perverse conversation and actions. It causes lapses in judgment and direction. It wounds and when it's finished, it, like all other sins, brings forth death. Isn't alcohol a wonderful thing!

Ahasuerus sat on his throne with all the princes, nobles, servants, and the other invited guests, and they were all intently looking at him to see what he was going to do about this spousal insurrection. The pressure was immense. Vashti refused to be brought out as the result of the king's poor judgment, sparked by his merry heart to be made a spectacle out of. She would not have hundreds of drunken men gawking at her beauty with lustful eyes and repulsive expressions.

What to do? The king gathered his advisors and asked them what was he to do about this? He had been shamed and disrespected by the queen whose behavior, as determined by the counselors, could not and should not be tolerated.

After all, as James Brown once sang "It's a man's world." They determined that it was not the king's fault, no, the blame lies with Vashti. It was all her fault for refusing to be reduced to a piece of eye candy.

Upon consultation, they decided the thing to do was to make an example out of Vashti. After all, she was the queen, the first lady, the female face of the Persian Empire. She needed to be put in her place, thus showing all the other women of the empire that standing up for personal respect and dignity as a woman would not be tolerated—no, not in this empire. I feel that Vashti quite possibly could be the godmother of the modern-day women's rights movement, although most women in the movement have probably never heard of her!

The King and his advisors had come up with a plan to prevent "uppity" women from inspiring other women who might have the propensity to get uppity as well. Who better to be set as an example for uppity behavior that would not be tolerated than the queen? Their reasoning was that if they could squelch her independent and rebellious attitude, no other women in the kingdom would dare think to rise up against their husbands and demand to be honored and treated with respect. Crazy, huh? It didn't take long and Vashti was made an example of. Banished. Gone. Ancient history.

With letters sent out to all the provinces of Persia detailing the crime and banishment of Vashti, fear would certainly be struck in the hearts of women everywhere. They were "put in their place" thus removing any threat of having a woman in this kingdom having thoughts for herself.

THE PARTIES OVER

Well, well, well. When Ahasuerus' heart was a little less merry and he had some time to think about what he had done, regret set in. He realized that he and his counselors were wrong. He was sorry for what he'd done to Vashti. He missed her and wished that she could return.

I have discovered that wisdom and alcohol cannot share the same venue. I think one of the most ridiculous and hypocritical statements I have ever heard goes like this, "drink responsibly." Excuse me??? Is there such a thing? There is being responsible and then there is drinking, but there is no such thing as responsible drinking. That's a myth.

When one is chosen, the other is forfeited. I've often said that you'll never see wisdom wearing a tee-shirt that says "I'm with stupid." We must understand that stupidity does what it does because it has stupid anointing it to do stupid things. Alcohol is great at magnifying stupidity.

When the alcohol-induced fog had lifted and the king could see clearly again; when the elephant finally removed its foot from off of his head and returned to the zoo; wisdom returned, and his heart desired to have Vashti back in the palace at his side. He would have sought reconciliation with her except for the fact that Persian law would not allow him to. In the Persian Empire, once a law had been decreed, it could not be canceled or even altered—not even by the king who established it.

Well at times like this there was only one thing that could be done. Find a new queen. This is what often happens when couples have a falling out.

Instead of working toward reconciliation and restoration, they begin to look for an easy exit, and unfortunately, they never have to look far to find one.

JUST GET A NEW ONE

The servants of Ahasuerus suggested that he send out teams of royal scouts to go into every city in the provinces of Persia and round up all the young, beautiful virgins for the king's inspection. There would be one chosen to replace Vashti out of the hundreds "lucky" enough to be selected as a candidate.

Upon selection, the lucky girl would be forcibly removed from her home and family and whisked off to Shushan by the king's royal scout team where they would be housed and given fragrant soaps and expensive perfumes to bathe in. After all, who would want to sit next to a smelly princess all day while conducting kingdom business? These young ladies also had access to the finest in modern day women's royal apparel, as well as their choice or jewelry made of breathtakingly beautiful and precious stones, gold, and silver. They had unlimited access to all they wanted and needed. They were allowed to choose their outfits and accessories, and they were able to keep all that they had chose to accomplish their "One Night with the King."

I can imagine that sort of a beauty pageant kind of atmosphere had taken over in the house where the king's women resided. I can only imagine what a chaotic endeavor it must have been for Hegai, the king's chamberlain, as he tried to oversee, organize, instruct, and direct them.

SHOPPING IS NOT FOR THE FAINT OF HEART

Like any good husband who doesn't mind a good flesh-peeling now and then, I have been clothes shopping with Val. Normally, when 'we' go shopping, I get a cup of coffee and find a bench to sit on that is close to the dressing room so I can assure her of how good she looks in whatever it is that she comes out and models for me.

I have witnessed her take an armload of clothes and go into a dressing room and, although I only saw her enter the room, I would have bet money (if

I was of that sort) that there had to have been more women in the room other than Val. Blouses, skirts, tops, dresses, jeans, and slacks; flying up and flying out.

There have been times during these dressing room frenzies that I have played William Tell Overture in my mind as I have witnessed her plow through her armload of various articles of clothing like a tornado plowing through a trailer park and scattering its contents chaotically throughout the area.

I have seen her as she opens the door and exits the dressing room with arms empty and having left various articles of clothing littered around the dressing room area only to come over to where I am sitting (minding my own business) and exclaim in total exasperation that nothing fits! It is then that I take another sip of my coffee and realize that I am not getting out of there any time soon. I am in for a long, fun-filled day of shopping, and a little more of my flesh is peeled and has fallen to the ground…

It was into this environment that a young girl named Hadassah, who was called Esther, had entered. She, like all the other young and beautiful girls that had been chosen, was placed in this house, but she was not like all the other girls. Her mother and father had died, and she went to live with her cousin, Mordecai, who raised her from youth.

Esther watched as the other girls grabbed the soaps and perfumes that appealed to their senses. She watched them as they went wildly through the racks of beautiful and elegant designer gowns, dresses, and jewelry. Then, there was the shoes! O, the shoes!! Rows and rows of every kind of shoe, in every kind of style, in every color, and for every occasion. Forgive me, but in my mind, I see these girls with a 'take no prisoners' attitude pushing and shoving one another, exhibiting behavior that would make some Black Friday brawls seem dull and boring.

PRESENCE CONNECTED TO PURPOSE RELEASES FAVOR

Esther refused to be engaged in all of this. She didn't have to. Because the presence of God was connected to her purpose. God had given her favor with the king's chamberlain. Divine favor is always the result of presence connected to purpose. This kind of favor will create an atmosphere in which it will announce you instead of you having to announce yourself.

Esther was not only beautiful, she was elegant. She was well mannered, chaste, proper, and well presented. Her outward beauty was a testimony of her inward purity and godly character. She was meek and gentle, with a quiet spirit. She had the presence of the Lord that had been with her from childhood although she probably never realized it. The presence had led her to this place, the place where she would realize her purpose, discover its connection with His presence, and enable her to complete her purpose which was to save her people from a madman named Haman, who was bent on Jewish genocide.

Protocol for entering Ahasuerus' presence would not allow these women, as beautiful as they were, to just come in off the street and enter the king's presence as they were. Protocol required that they bathe in a small pool filled with aloes, ointments, oils, spices, and perfumes. This process took twelve months to complete. It was a time of purification, a cleaning, that removed all odors from these women that may not have been pleasant or attractive to the king and his senses.

From this point, they would dress in whatever they had chosen to wear as they presented themselves, and then they were led into the king's presence. After spending the evening with the king, they were taken to a second house where they remained and would never come again into the king's presence unless they were called by him to come for a visit.

One by one these young ladies would enter in the evening, exit in the morning, and remain uncalled indefinitely. No doubt Esther observed the women that went before her as they prepared themselves. She would see them exit the house and take the walk from their living quarters to the king's chambers. The presence that was with Esther's purpose had given her favor and favor caused Hagai to position Esther for the greatness of purpose completed.

WHAT PLEASES THE KING?

When it came time for Esther to present herself before Ahasuerus, instead of browsing through the racks of clothing, the display cases of jewelry, the seemingly endless selection of shoes, and choosing what she thought was good and desirable, the presence of the Lord that was with Esther gave her the wisdom to take the time to stop and ask Hagai what it was that would please the king. Although it is clear from the Book of Esther that at the beginning she did not know what her purpose was, the presence caused her to understand that somehow she was not in this place for just her own benefit.

It was not an accident. She might have begun to realize that she was there for a greater cause; greater than herself and her future. She might not have known it all, but she was now at the place where it would begin to unfold before her very eyes. And presence would make sure that she was prepared to meet the challenges that she was about to encounter.

In Ch.2:15, the Bible implies that Esther asked Hagai what it was that would please the king and she asked for nothing more. Her desire was not like that of the other girls—which was to please themselves first and then pleasing the king. Esther's desire was to please the king first, because she understood that if the king was pleased with her then she would have his heart and if she had his heart, she would have all of him.

As Esther took the now infamous walk from the house of the women to the chamber of the king that so many had taken before her, she captured the attention of everyone that saw her. She was stunning, not overdone nor underdone. It was as if the eyes of those who saw her had a mind of their own, and would not allow themselves to be turned away from her until she was completely out of their view.

As she approached the king's chamber, she was presented by the chamberlain. When she appeared, the king was so captivated by her that he nearly fell off of his throne. It was love at first sight. None of the women that came before Esther had moved the heart of the king like she did. He wasted no time in placing a crown upon her head and positioning her as his queen.

Ahasuerus once again made a feast for all the princes, nobles, servants, and some common folk in Shushan where he presented Esther as his queen. This time, however, he had learned a valuable lesson and would not make the same mistake twice. Esther would never be called upon to be the center of attention for the viewing pleasure of a bunch of drunken, lustful, and repulsive men.

A PARALLEL TRUTH

I believe that there is a parallel truth from the story of Esther; something powerful that we must see and understand. This truth is simply this: Just as there was protocol to come into Ahasuerus' presence, there is protocol to come into the presence of the King of kings and Lord of lords.

We must understand that Esther here is a type of the Church, and just as Esther could not come into the king's presence without protocol and preparation, we cannot come into the presence of our King without following His Kingdom's protocol and preparation. We cannot come into the presence of our God dirty, smelling like the world, wearing filthy garments, and ill-mannered. I often say that you can't touch holy things with dirty hands and you can't go into holy places with dirty feet.

Esther took the time to prepare herself for the king's presence, and we as the Church need to understand that we cannot come into the presence of our King any less prepared. Esther was not interested in 'One night with the king', she wanted a lifetime with him. It must be the same with us. We cannot allow our desire to be that of one night, but of a lifetime, and yet not just in this lifetime, but a desire to be in His presence that transcends this life and continues into the eternal.

Esther relied on Hagai with whom she had favor with to help her to understand the protocol and how to know what it was that pleased the king to ensure that she would have his favor and his heart.

In this, Hagai is a type of the Holy Spirit, who as Hagai dwelt with the king's women, also dwells with us, in us, and favors us—showing us what we must do to enter the presence of the King of Glory. The problem is not the lack of purpose, we all have purpose. WE were born with it. I believe that purpose and anointing are very similar. An anointing gives us our purpose and empowers us to complete it. Saint or sinner, righteous or wicked, everybody is anointed. Wicked people have a wicked anointing on them that enables them to do wicked things. Conversely, righteous people have a righteous anointing on them that enables them to do righteous things. A wicked anointing will never produce a righteous thing—and a righteous anointing will cause the righteous to never want to do wicked things. The real problem comes when we have purpose, but lack presence.

Everything that exists in our world today has a reason for its existence. If it ceases to have a reason, it ceases to exist. We can think of things in our lifetime that, at one time, had purpose. It had a reason for its existence, but as time, trends, technology, and economies change and move forward, has ceased to be so, therefore, it has ceased to exist. One thing is for certain, the Church of Jesus Christ will always have a purpose, and because of that it will never cease to exist. The question will never be one of purpose, but it will be one of presence.

Presence connected to purpose took a young orphaned girl from nothing, gave her favor, and positioned her as queen in the most powerful and influential kingdom of this time period. Imagine what His presence connected to your purpose could position you to accomplish!

For us in the Church, being purpose driven is not enough—we must be presence driven.

Chapter Ten

Presence, Purpose, and Faith to Complete

HEBREWS CHAPTER 11 IS ONE of my personal favorites. It is the only chapter of the Bible that is open-ended. By that, I mean it has not yet been completed, but it is still being written. We may never know of them or read about their story in this life: but every day, hundreds of names, along with their stories from around the world, are added to the roster of those whose purpose remained connected to His presence. The result of their faithfulness to God was that they were able to believe Him for great and mighty things. Miracles, signs, and wonders were and are still being accomplished for His Kingdom and glory. Hebrews 11 details several heroes of the faith, many of whom at some point had purpose and presence but, for various reasons, lost the presence. But before it was all said and done, presence was regained and reconnected with their purpose; and they achieved great things for God that has had lasting and eternal value. Hebrews eleven also talks about those who refused to allow their purpose to become disconnected from His presence. Their determination produced faith to complete their purpose. It has left us a legacy that encourages us to maintain the connection of presence and purpose, which produces faith in us to complete the calling of God for our lives.

The writer of Hebrews begins writing this chapter by encouraging the reader to possess, and exercise faith. Faith is the key in retaining the connection between presence and purpose. When presence connects with purpose, the result is faith in completing our calling. He states that those who have gone before us obtained a "good report" (they were deemed a faithful witness of God) through the possession of faith and exercising it.

According to Heb.1:3, presence with purpose came together with the Word of Almighty God. And through the power of His Word, He created the heavens, the earth, and all they contain. The writer says that they were 'formed' or made complete by the power of His Word.

All throughout the Scriptures we see that the power of God is the Word of God. Psalm 138:2 says that He has magnified His Word above His name.

There are words that are higher than yours: there are words that are higher than mine. Let me give you this example.

Have you ever told someone you would do something or meet them somewhere, or attend an event, only to have another word spoken (something else that came up and couldn't be avoided) that kept you from fulfilling what you said you would do? We all have, haven't we? It happens because there are "words" higher than ours, and we are left to bow our word to theirs. Although this happens to us frequently, it has never happened to God because there is no word higher than His! This is why we pray His Word and not ours.

God spoke through the Prophet Isaiah concerning the power of His Word in Ch55:11. The Lord declared that the Word that proceeds out of His mouth would not return to him empty; it will accomplish what He pleases and prosper in what He sends it to do. King David said in Psalm 33:9 that God spoke and what He said was done; He commanded and what He commanded to stand...stands. The secret to maintaining the connection of presence and purpose is to consistently declare and apply His Word concerning your purpose, which produces faith to complete your calling. The Apostle Paul said in Rom.10:17 that faith comes by hearing the Word of God. As we hear the Word, faith in that Word is produced within us.

THE CARPENTER

I don't believe that it was a coincidence that Jesus was in the carpentry business before He stepped fully into His ministry while here on earth. It is His very nature to construct, restore, repair, revive, renew, refinish, and reuse.

Throughout the Gospels, we see Jesus, the wise master builder, taking out his tools and constructing, repairing, and reusing men and women He came in contact with. The same Word that was powerful enough to frame the universe and hold it in order was the same Word that framed the life of tax collectors, fishermen, doctors, lawyers, prostitutes, adulterers, widows, and children. It framed salvation for the lost, healing for the sick, miracles for the broken, deliverances for the captives, strength for the weak, unburdening for the oppressed, justification for the guilty, and freedom for the imprisoned.

Jesus took the hammer of His Word and framed wisdom and understanding, knowledge, the way, truth, and eternal life. He framed an anointing which He released in those who were "built" by Him. His Word framed grace, peace, mercy, love, hope, help, comfort, joy, Kingdom prosperity, and the list goes on and on.

Equally fascinating, I find the same presence that empowered the Word to do all of these things still has the power to frame your world and hold it all together—because the Word, like the Blood, will never lose its power!

I love the words of Psalm 127:1-2, where David writes, "Unless the Lord builds the house, they labor in vain that build it. It is vain for you to rise up early, and to sit up late." These verses declare that God alone can build an eternal house, and that He alone is eternally able to keep what He has built.

Apostle Paul said in 2Cor.5:1, Jesus has constructed our house and our lives in the world as a tent. A tent is symbolic of our lives here on earth as temporal and transitory. This tent will one day wear out and be of no further use. Because of this, Paul continued to say that Jesus is in heaven, framing us an eternal house. Jesus is building testaments of permanence. David said that we would dwell in the Lord's permanent house forever.

HEAVEN'S HALL OF FAME

I want to highlight with written ovation those from Hebrews 11 whose purpose, regardless of the adversity they faced, stayed connected to the presence and what they were able to do for the God they so faithfully served.

ABEL THE ACCEPTED AND RESPECTED BY GOD

Presence with purpose produced faith in Abel that caused him to offer a greater sacrifice than Cain. As I stated in Ch.1, I believe that what caused Abel's offering to be accepted by God when He rejected Cain's was their heart's attitude in offering the gift.

ENOCH THE POWER WALKER

Presence with purpose produced faith in a man named Enoch, whom the Bible said walked with (fellowshipped with, followed after) God. In the genealogical record of Adam and Eve's descendants recorded in Gen.5, Enoch and Noah are the only ones that Moses says 'walked with God' before the flood: and Abel, Enoch, and Noah were the only ones referred to in the Bible as being righteous in that period.

There are a few things that we know about Enoch from Scriptures. We know that he was married, had children, walked with God, and was a prophet. We know that he had purpose and he had presence, which produced in him a strong faith that pleased God. We know that Enoch went for a walk with God one day, and he never returned. The Bible says in Gen.5:24, "And Enoch walked with God; and was not, because God took (seized, carried) him." In Heb.11, the writer says that God's presence with Enoch's purpose caused him to not see death but to be translated by God into heaven. The Word 'translated' means to be transported and to change sides. Gen.5:24 and Heb.11:5 teach us that because presence connected with Enoch's purpose, he was transported from earth to heaven without seeing death. He changed sides from the earthy to the heavenly.

Presence with purpose produced faith that created a powerful legacy for those who in the coming generations would walk with, fellowship with, and follow after God: and it left behind a testimony for us of a man whose walk with God pleased Him. O, to live a life that pleases God! It is possible, you know!

A FAITH THAT PLEASES GOD

I love the fact that God never leaves us to guess or to try and figure out how we are going to accomplish the calling He has placed on our lives. Verse six of Heb.11 is kind of an intermission statement that declares faith in His presence and confidence in His purpose for our life is what pleases God. We must believe that He will reward those who seek His presence to complete their purpose. From Genesis to Revelation, we can find examples of this for us to imitate and follow.

www.noahandsons.com

The finest name in ship design, construction, and shipping logistics. "When it simply must arrive, Noah and Sons Delivers"

Heb.11:7 tells us that the presence of God was with Noah, and with presence came relationship, and relationship connected presence with purpose. It was Noah's relationship that released presence. The same holds true for us today. Our relationship with God will always release His presence and connect it with the purpose for which we are called.

Gen.6 records God's plan to judge the sin of mankind by flooding the earth. The presence and passion for it that had once been with Adam and Eve had long since been forgotten. In Noah's day (like in ours), it was even fought against. This was an obvious grievance unto the heart of God. He concluded that the only way to rid the earth of such rebellion and disobedience was to destroy all those who had violated His established law.

The same words the Prophet Isaiah used in Ch.60 prophetically describing the spiritual and moral climate of a future day and time could have been used to describe the spiritual and moral climate that was prevalent in

Noah's day as well. Isaiah said in verse two, "Darkness shall (a statement of fact) cover the earth, and gross darkness the people."

A spiritual and moral darkness has now covered the earth and a significant percentage of its people in our day, just as it did during Noah's time. It placed the people in a darkness that became impossible to navigate through.

I remember several years ago; Val and I went to Uganda to speak at a pastor/church leadership conference. We were in the bush, and the bush was in the middle of nowhere. There was no phone, no light no motor car, not a single luxury (Okay, there was one car. That's how we got there). I remember walking from the church building furnished with one light over the pulpit and was powered by a generator. The seating was 2X6 boards that sat on cinderblock. The church was about 200 yards from a minus four-star hotel called the Volcano Hotel and Arcade. There were no volcanoes, and there certainly was no arcade at this hotel.

I remember leaving the church after the evening service and Val and I were trying to make it from the church to the hotel. In the pitch-black darkness of the night, we were navigating the dirt trail from the church to the hotel. The path was very uneven. It went uphill and was filled with rocks that stuck up partially from the ground, out just enough to trip you pretty good. There were potholes, mounds, dips…and lots of rocks. You literally could not see your hand in front of your face. Our only hope of successfully completing our journey from the church to the hotel was a torch. A torch was what the locals called a flashlight. It was in these times that I could understand and appreciate Jesus' words concerning lighting a candle and receiving the benefit of its light. I am pretty sure that we would have eventually made it from the church to the hotel but with the torch, we arrived without any physical damage.

I love the words of Gen.6:8, where Moses wrote, "But Noah found grace in the eyes of the Lord." Presence connected to purpose, which resulted in the grace of God being poured out on Noah like a fragrant ointment that was sent to aid, strengthen, and preserve him. Even amidst all the wickedness,

Noah was still a man that the Bible said was just; and like Enoch, Noah walked with God.

There are modern-day Noah's, you know? People who live in the same climate of spiritual and moral decline as that of Noah's day but, like Noah, are determined to walk with God, and this determination enables them to possess the testimony of the just. Like the original, these modern-day Noah's have also heard the Word of God pronouncing a day of judgment and by faith have built unto themselves an Ark of Salvation, who is Jesus.

JOSEPH: DARING TO LIVE THE DREAM

Jacob's youngest son, Joseph, is the main focus to whom Hebrews 11:22 is dedicated to. Genesis Chapters 37-50 tells us of his story. Presence and purpose were with Joseph from a young age. This can be seen in the prophetic dreams that God had given him: dreams that bred conflict between him and his brothers to the point that some of his brothers wanted nothing more than to see their youngest brother dead.

When it comes to dreamers, there are two things I know. There will always be those who dare to dream and those who hate them for it. History is completely filled with examples of men and women who dared to dream and those who hated them for it. And history in the waiting will be, as well. Both will share the same future stage. Some will be celebrated, while the others will be bowing at their feet.

It is not uncommon at all for those who have purpose but lack presence to hate or be jealous of those who have them both, even when they are in the same family. After all, Jesus said in Matt.10:36 that 'a man's enemies will be they of his own household.'

Sometimes, it could be diagnosed as sibling rivalry. But maybe, just like in the cases of Joseph and his brothers, Cain and Abel, Esau and Jacob, Isaac and Ishmael, and David and his brothers—purpose with the presence had fostered envy and jealousy that manifested in them a malicious hatred for each other, pitting sibling against sibling.

God's presence connected to Joseph's purpose kept him through his brothers' verbal and physical attacks, hate, and jealousy. Presence connected with purpose kept Joseph when some of his brothers wanted to kill him. It kept him when they threw him in a pit. It kept him when he was sold as a slave. It kept him when Potiphar bought him. When Potiphar's wife tried to seduce him and then lied about it, it kept him. It kept him when he was thrown in prison and promoted to prison administrator by the warden. It enabled him to interpret the Pharaoh's dream. And it stayed with him even after he was released from prison and was promoted to a position where he was only subject to the Pharaoh himself.

If there was ever a man that could have used his circumstances as an excuse to separate his purpose from the Lord's presence, Joseph would have been that man. But he refused. Instead, he was determined to allow His presence to be so interwoven in the fabric of his soul that it became impossible to see where the presence began and where his purpose ended. God's presence and Joseph's purpose blended together until they had become inseparably united.

I believe that the Lord gave young Joseph dreams, and they became the benchmark of his purpose. The Lord caused him to understand their meaning because He knew that it would take this kind of certainty to carry Joseph through the hardship's and betrayals he would endure to possess and retain the faith necessary to complete his purpose.

But the one thing that I desire to emphasize here is that we can find the source of Joseph's success and prosperity in Gen. 39:2: "And the Lord was with Joseph." This means that the Lord was everywhere Joseph was. No matter where Joseph went, the Lord was 'Jehovah Shammah': The Lord who is present. Because the Lord was with Joseph, he was a prosperous man.

Possessions, wealth, fame, social status, talents, or accomplishments do not determine real success. One day, all of these things will fade away into the annals of ancient history and will soon be forgotten. Success is not dependent on circumstance, education, birthright, or where you were born. It's not the product of being at the right place at the right time. It's certainly not the product of dumb luck. True success is defined within the statement of Moses when he wrote "And the Lord was WITH Joseph." If the Lord is with you, nothing that's against you will prosper. Apostle Paul understood this principle when he wrote in Romans 8:31, "If God be for us (with us), who can be against us?" If God prepares you a table in the presence of your enemies, which one of them can stop you from eating? David wrote in Psalm46:1 "God is our refuge and strength, a very present help in trouble." The term "very present" means that God was your refuge and strength before you stepped into trouble—He'll still be your refuge and strength while you're in trouble—and He'll be your refuge and strength when you come out on the other side of trouble. Bless His name!

Joseph believed this. Do you? Maintaining the Lord's presence with your purpose as well as your prosperity and all that it contains depends on it.

THE HARLOT AND THOSE MEN IN THE PARLOR...

A friend of mine once said to me, "Paul, God is not as concerned about where you've been and what you've done as He is with where you're going and what you'll do."

There is no testament more fitting of this than in the story concerning a prostitute named Rahab. Heb.11:31 talks about this lady of the evening who lived in the city of Jericho. Her story is found in Joshua Ch.2.

Now before we get too judgmental of her or the Lord for choosing her, we must understand that before we were born again and our relationship restored unto God by Jesus Christ, we were like a spiritual Rahab. The Apostle Paul makes this abundantly clear in 1Cor.6:16-20. This is also illustrated in the theme of Prophet Hosea's story, where his wife, Gomer, also happened to be a harlot. Thankfully for us, God is still in the business of redeeming prostitutes of all kinds.

I have come to understand that God can use anyone or anything to complete His purpose. He used a donkey to rebuke a prophet. He used a star to announce the birth of Jesus. He used another donkey to carry the Word (who is Jesus) into the city of Jerusalem. He used a rooster to convict a disciple. God used many people, the righteous and the wicked alike, to fulfill His purpose. We could fill pages with example after example of this. The real goal is not to just be used by God, but to be wanted by Him. You see, Mark wrote in Ch.3:13 that Jesus went up into a mountain and He called unto Himself all those whom He wanted. Do I desire to be used by God? Absolutely, yes! Do I desire more to be wanted by Him? Absolutely, yes, I do!! O, not just to be used…but to be wanted!

There are several things that I find interesting about this story, not the least of which is that God connected His presence with a Gentile harlot to carry out His purpose for His people—to the extent that she became a part of the genealogical ancestry of Jesus. But then again, Jesus was never afraid to be identified with the outcast and forgotten. Rahab was King David's great-great-grandmother!

I am reminded once again of the Lord's words to the Prophet Samuel when He was removing Saul from the throne and replacing him with David. 1Sam.16:7 says, "For the Lord does not see as men see." What the men of Jericho saw was a harlot, a prostitute, but what God saw was a young lady that would believe Him, and it would be her faith in Him that would cause her entire family to be saved. That's obvious.

What may be overlooked is the fact that even though she didn't know it, she had the presence of God that was waiting patiently for her to discover His presence and her purpose.

A good illustration of this is found in the story of Elijah and Elisha.

The Bible says in 1 Kings19:19-21 that Elijah came to where Elisha was plowing in a field. Verse nineteen says that Elijah threw his mantle on Elisha, signifying that a transference of the anointing that was on Elijah was about to be transferred to Elisha. Elisha requests permission from Elijah to set his affairs in order and say good bye to his family and his way of life.

In the KJV Bible, Elijah's response to Elisha, at face value, seems a little harsh. It reads, "Go back again: for what have I done unto thee?" But what Elijah was really saying here to Elisha was, "Do what you have to do, and when you're ready, I'll be here waiting for you." God is such a patient God! He is a very methodical God. He never gets nervous or anxious. He has everything in control.

In this, I find such grace from God because that's how He is, isn't it? He calls us, throws an anointing on us, to complete His calling on us: but sometimes it happens that when He is ready, we're not quite there yet. Some of us find ourselves saying to the Lord, "Let me do this" or "I first need to do that." And the patience of God allows Him to wait on us. But when we come back to where He called us, it is time for us to take up our cross and follow Him. The Lord was waiting on Rahab. Did He like or approve of her lifestyle, No! But His patience allowed Him looked past it, not excusing it, but looked past it, and to see this day. Aren't you so very grateful that He patiently waited for you!

The presence of God that waited on Rahab connected with her purpose one night when Joshua sent some men out on reconnaissance mission into the city of Jericho. Her faith in Israel's God was manifested through the confidence of her words to these men. She knew it was not a matter of (if) they would conquer the city, but when. It was at this moment, God connected His presence with Rahab's purpose and the result was faith that enabled her to hide these men and aide their escape. Presence connected with purpose, produced a faith that saved her and her family from impending doom. It also produced a faith that allowed her to go beyond the saving of her family and into the fullness of her anointing. Presence connected to purpose has caused the children of a thousand generation to rise up and call her "blessed."

ENTERING THE HALL OF CHAMPIONS

Hebrews 4:12 says that the Word of God is living; and as such, it has the power to give life and to sustain it—both physical and spiritual. Paul said that if the same Spirit that raised Jesus from the dead is in us, then, we will also be raised. Since the Word of God is living, it has a pulse: by this I mean that there are Scripture passages that as you read them, it seems like there is a shift in intensity, rhythm, cadence, etc. For me, Psalm six is a perfect example of this. Psalm 6 is entitled "Third Prayer of Distress." You may recall from a previous chapter I said that distress means to feel like you're being pulled apart. Maybe like me, you're old enough to remember that boy doll called "Stretch Armstrong." The commercials showed a boy pulling Stretch's arms in complete opposite directions, and when the boy released the tension, Stretch would go back into his natural state. This is a great example of stress. Distress comes from two words meaning to pull or to stretch apart.

We've all felt like this at some point in our lives. Adversity comes and it causes us to feel like we are being mentally or emotionally pulled apart. Psalm six starts out slow, heavy, and sorrowful: but in verse eight, you can feel a shift, you can feel the pulse change. It increases in intensity, cadence, and attitude.

I believe that this is what happens in Heb.11. There is a constant building as example after example is laid out for our inspection and encouragement to maintain the Lord's presence with our purpose and producing faith to complete our calling. I can feel it as it increases in intensity and drive: and by the time you reach verse 32 of this 11th chapter, the writer moves into a fever pitch.

He begins to fire off name after name. Gideon, Barak, Samson, Jephthah, David, and Samuel: he references Daniel, Shadrach, Meshach, and Abed-nego, as well as Elijah, Elisha, and many, many more. O, I get excited just thinking about it!

Then the writer of Hebrews shifts gears, and begins to describe what they accomplished when the presence of God connected with the purpose of these godly men. The subdued kingdoms, lived righteous lives before the Lord, possessed promises, stopped the mouths of lions, quenched the violence of fire, escaped the edge of the sword, out of weakness were made strong, waxed valiant in battle, defeated enemy armies causing them to retreat, and resurrected the dead!

But these, Oh, these were the more glamorous stories in the Bible—they're the ones we all love to sing about and shout over. These are the stories that make us jump to our feet, run around the church high-fiving each other as though our team just scored a touchdown; or hit a walk off grand slam to win the World Series. They're the ones we confess, profess, claim, quote, cross our eyes, legs, toes, and fingers over, and hope for. They make us want to strap on our dancing shoes and cut a little rug as we claim their victories for our own.

Many times when we read these verses when we come to verse 34, we come to a screeching halt and stop here at the place of these euphoric and victorious testimonies: and we treat the latter verses as though they don't exist or don't apply to us. The latter verses of Hebrews 11 don't even belong in the theology of some churches. The problem is that even though we may stop at verse 34, the writer of Hebrews 11, didn't. After we've shouted our way to the pinnacle of "Mount Victory," in the second half of verse thirty-five, he pushes us off the cliff with his next statement. "How's that" you say?

We would love to stop there in victory lane, wouldn't we? We would love to confess—no fire will burn me, no lion will eat me, no enemy will defeat me, death won't touch me, my strength in the Lord—and it's all Scriptural! But it doesn't stop there. He continued on down the other side of the mountain he spent thirty-four verses climbing up.

Sometimes, and we don't like to talk about it because it's an inconvenient truth, or it doesn't fit in our theology: but sometimes when the presence connects with our purpose, it causes us to go down a road that is a little less than victorious, joyous, desirable, and shout-worthy: but nonetheless, necessary and meaningful. See. The same verse that declared the dead were raised also says that others were tortured. "Say what?" "Wait. Did you say, t-t-t-tortured!?" Yes, tortured.

I love the story in John twenty-one of Jesus walking with Peter along the shore of the Sea of Galilee. Jesus just had Peter confess his love for Him as many times as he denied that he even knew Him. And now, they are walking together discussing future events in Peter's life. Jesus said to him "Peter, when you were young you dressed yourself, you went where you wanted to go, and you did what you wanted to do. But, when you get older, someone else will dress you, bind you, and they will lead you where you don't want to go: and you'll have to do something that you'd really rather not have to do."

Jesus was telling Peter that there was coming a time when he would be martyred for his testimony of Him. Now, all of this time, John was following Jesus and Peter, but he was following a few steps behind them, but close enough that he could hear Jesus' and Peter's conversation. Peter turned around, and looked at John. His reason for doing so was that it was getting a hot in the kitchen, and he wanted to take that kettle off the stove and let it cool down a minute. So Peter asks Jesus "What about this guy?" Jesus lovingly said to Peter as He moved the kettle back over the fire "Peter, you let me worry about him: you just take care of Peter."

Can you imagine what Peter's response would have been if Jesus had told this to him when they first met? "Follow Me." Jesus said to Peter, and then He continued "O, by the way Pete, when you're an older guy, you're going to be bound, imprisoned, and crucified upside down…for following Me. Well, come on now, chin up, off we go!"

Upon receiving this little almost insignificant piece of information, I can see Peter saying to Jesus "Well, cool. But you know, I…I just remembered. My wife really needs me to, um, clean the leaves out the rain gutters. You, you go on ahead, and I…I'll catch up with You." Peter would have turned and ran and never followed Jesus. And if the Lord told me, or you that in the beginning of our walk with Him, we probably would have ran too.

Why? Because at that point in the relationship, we couldn't have handled that heavy of a revelation. For you who are married, think about when you first met your spouse. On the outside you were polished and appeared to be in order. Nothing out of place, nothing suspect showing. You said everything right, you did everything right. You put on a performance that was worthy of an Oscar for best actor or actress. And you only took out of your heart for their inspection what the relationship could handle. Because you knew, that if your future spouse really knew who you were and what you were like, they like Peter, would have excused themselves hailed a taxi, and you would have never seen them again.

But as your relationship grew and trust was being built, you could feel more comfortable in exposing a little bit more of your heart's contents. The deeper the relationship, the deeper we reach into our heart and lay more of its contents up on the table for each other to inspect.

Some people surely don't understand this, and the result is that they literally run off the very person they are trying to build a relationship with. No doubt this would have happened with Peter had Jesus told him this too soon.

THE VICTORIOUS WHOSE NAMES ARE KNOWN ONLY IN HEAVEN

Some heroes of the faith and their accomplishments have been documented throughout the centuries and are known among the believer and in some cases the non-believer alike. But then there are the not-so-famous faithful, the honorable but unnamed great men and women of God, who no doubt make up the majority of those who were less known, but no less important in contribution to the advancing of the Kingdom of God and for His glory. They may be less known but no less victorious than those who became household names and synonymous with the testimonies and legacies of an overcomer.

Hebrews 11:36-38 reveals this record of the unnamed overcomers whose purpose connected to His presence, caused them to remain faithful while being mocked, beaten, bound, imprisoned, stoned, sawn in two, tested, slain by the sword, hated, and abused. His presence and their purpose preserved them when they were forced into being vagabonds in want of food, clothing, and shelter. It held them as they were being afflicted, persecuted, and considered evil, vile, and worthless...subhuman. Presence with purpose was a compass that directed them when self-preservation pressed them into being nomad's, wandering through deserts and mountains; and only finding shelter in dens and caves.

As I was writing this and looking at Heb.11:39, the Lord showed me two things. First, the second group whose testimony was a bit less desirable for most of us, obtained a good report just like the Abraham's Enoch's, Moses', David's, and Gideon's. The second thing that He showed me was that the same Lord that was on the mountain top with the Noah's, the Samson's, the Joseph's, and the Samuel's, was the same Lord that was in the valleys with these nameless (but whose names has been recorded in heaven) faithful men and women of God. They, all together, have obtained a good report and have left an example of what can be accomplished for the Kingdom of God when His presence stays connected together with our purpose: and produces a faith in us that enables us to complete our calling.

As great as these men and women of God were and as powerful of a legacy that they all have left behind, their story of presence connected with purpose has been written and completed: its' over and done. But if you're reading this, yours is still being written. The question then becomes— whether we're well known in his world or unknown; named or unnamed, how will your story end? May it be ever Presence Driven. The peace of Christ you. All for His glory!

Epilogue

THERE ARE SO MANY MORE examples throughout the Bible of people whose purpose connected with the presence of the Lord. Through His presence, they were able to accomplish amazing things that inspire and challenge us to always keep our purpose connected to His presence, and, in turn, we can expect great things. These are heroes of the faith whose exploits remain a testimony to God's awesome power and glory, such as Gideon, Elijah, Elisha, Joshua, Samuel, the prophets, and the Apostles. The list could go on and on.

Having the presence means that we have His Spirit, His face, His favor: we have Him with us, enabling us to accomplish the purpose He has given us. It means that He has accepted, equipped, positioned, and anointed us. Being connected with His presence means that He has focused His attention on us and will go before, beside, behind, above, and beneath us. Having the presence means that we have the right and the responsibility to take up ownership of His Word and declare it as if it were our own. Psalm 103:20 says, "Bless the Lord, all you His angels that excel in strength, that do His commandments, and listen carefully for His Word."

I understand this to mean that when I declare His Word concerning my purpose, it is not my voice that the angels hear because it's not my word that I am declaring. It is His Word, therefore, when I speak His Word in His name, even though it came from my mouth, what the angels hear is His Word, His voice, and they move to complete what has been spoken.

The Apostle Paul said in 1Cor.15:45 that Jesus is a life-giving Spirit. When we possess the presence declaring His Word, we, like Jesus, are a life-giving spirit: we release life to everything that should live and remain: our purpose should always be a living purpose producing abundant fruit.

Is it always easy? No. At times it is far from it. Those of us who have been around the Kingdom for a while understand that. But we also understand that even though it's not always going to be easy, it will always be worth it. Oh, just to hear Him say "Well done" should be the constant motivation of our purpose and determination to keep it connected to His presence.

It is not always easy. King David expressed this truth, in Psalm 16:11, when he wrote, "You will show me the path of life: in Your presence is fullness of joy; at Your right hand are pleasures forevermore."

I want you to see three things in this verse that I think are very important for us to understand as we maintain the connection of our purpose with His presence.

First, Israel's great King declared his confidence in God's ability and willingness to not only show him the path that leads to life, but to accompany him on the journey. The same applies to us. Jesus said to His disciples in Matt.28:20, "I Am with you always, even unto the end of the age." The Apostle Paul said in Heb.13:5, "For He has said, I will never leave you nor forsake you." This statement by Paul quoted from Josh.1:5 should serve as a strong encouragement for us in that no matter what we face on life's path, we will never be left to face it on our own; or to find our own way.

Psalm 119:105 tells us that His Word is a lamp unto our feet and a light to our pathway. "The Apostle John said in the first chapter of the Gospel that bears his name, that the Word, who is Jesus, is Light; and that He illuminates our path and guides us safely from where we are to where He is."

As long as we remain on this path, we can be assured that His presence will always remain connected to our purpose, that we will complete all that He has called us to do for His Kingdom and for His glory.

Second, David states, "In His presence, there is fullness of joy." I want you to notice that David did not say that in His purpose, there is fullness of joy; it is only in His presence. I can only speak for myself, but sometimes the purpose of God for the lives of His people—for my life, can at times seem to not be all that joyous.

We can find many examples of this throughout the Bible and in the lives of faithful saints around our world today as they endure trouble, trial, and tribulations. Sometimes our purpose can be defined using words such as difficult, pressing, hard, vexing, trying, turbulent, etc., but we have a promise from God; these things are light and momentary.

Purpose, at times, can seem to be more than we can overcome; and with just our own strength, we can be assured that it is impossible. Fortunately, we don't have to forge our own path with our own strength, but we can walk the path that He has made and walk it in His presence and His strength. Presence connected to purpose releases the fullness of joy that David writes about here in Psalm 16.

Finally, David declares that there are pleasures forevermore at the Father's right hand. David said that there is something that surpassed all that is beautiful, wonderful, marvelous, sweet, delightful, and valuable at the Father's right hand. The pleasure that David says is at the Father's right hand cannot be comprehended or experienced in its fullness in our present state.

So, what is this pleasure David refers to? Mark 16:19, Luke 22:69, Acts 2:33-34, 7:55-56, Rom.8:34, Eph.1:20, Col.3:1, Heb.1:3,13, 8:1, 10:12, and 1Pet.3:22 tells us that the pleasure at the right hand of the Father is...Jesus! Jesus is the pinnacle of all that is glorious and desired: and to those whose purpose remains connected to His presence, there is no greater pleasure, no greater joy, than Jesus.

My prayer and desire for you are that you would determine with a made-up mind to stay on the path, maintain the presence, and find the "evermore" pleasure that is Jesus and can only be found in His presence. The peace of Christ to you. All for His glory! Amen.

CPSIA information can be obtained
at www.ICGtesting.com
Printed in the USA
LVHW051823130323
741526LV00008B/831